Critical acclaim for *Gandhi*

later than those covered in [Gandhi's] autobiography." —*Crozer Quarterly*, Crozer Theological Seminary, Chester, Pennsylvania

"[This book] has special value. It is the work of an American Christian missionary who befriended Gandhi and regarded him as one of the few persons who have tried to live a Christian life." —*Political Science Quarterly*

"Dr. Jones is never dull." —*Christian Science Monitor*

". . . an informative and inspiring volume. Not only a perceptive biography of one of the most outstanding persons of the 20th century, but a commentary on some of the most crucial issues of our time. The church is in need of this message."—Maxie Dunnam, minister, Christ United Methodist Church, Memphis, Tennessee; formerly world editor, *The Upper Room*

"Martin Luther King, Jr., told me he owed a debt to my father for his book on Mahatma Gandhi. He had read many books on Gandhi, read his writings, but it was that particular book of my father's that had triggered his decision to use the method of . . . nonviolence in his civil rights movement for his people." —Eunice Jones Mathews, daughter of E. Stanley Jones

GANDHI

Portrayal of a Friend

E. STANLEY JONES

ABINGDON PRESS
Nashville

GANDHI:
PORTRAYAL OF A FRIEND

Published by Abingdon Press in 1993 as an Abingdon Classic.
Previously published under ISBN 0-697-13999-6,
and in 1948 under the title *Mahatma Gandhi—an Interpretation.*

93 94 95 96 97 98 99 00 01 02—10 9 8 7 6 5 4 3 2 1

Library of Congress Cataloging-in-Publication Data

Jones, E. Stanley (Eli Stanley), 1884–1973.
  [Mahatma Gandhi]
  Gandhi : portrayal of a friend / by E. Stanley Jones.
    p.   cm.—(Abingdon classics)
  Originally published: Mahatma Gandhi. Nashville : Stone & Pierce,
1948.
  ISBN 0-687-13870-1 (alk. paper)
  1. Gandhi, Mahatma, 1869–1948. 2. Statesman—India—Biography.
3. Nationalists—India—Biography. I. Title. II. Series.
  DS481.G3J67   1993
  954.03'5'092—dc20
[B]   92-38411
                                                                        CIP

MANUFACTURED IN THE UNITED STATES OF AMERICA

Foreword

THIS book was not an easy book to write—not for me. When the cable came from the publishers in America asking me to write the book, I put it aside as impossible. I never write a book by request. It must come as a result of an inner urge which I cannot put aside. I felt no such inner urge about this.

I have believed in and have loved Mahatma Gandhi through the years —in spite of differences. I have stood in sympathy with the Mahatma and have expressed that sympathy during the years when to do so was to open one to the charge of being the queer defending the queer, the off-center defending the eccentric. But to try to interpret such a complex character as he was—well, it was beyond me and wasn't my task. He was simple and yet very complex amid that simplicity. You thought you knew him, and then you didn't. It was intriguing. There was always something there that eluded your grasp, something that baffled you. And yet out of that many-sidedness which amounted to complexity, there arose simplicity, a unified character, simple and compelling. Could I interpret that? It was like trying to interpret Mount Everest. It is many-sided. It rises in simple grandeur, and yet there are subsidiary peaks, crevices, depths, plateaus, all contributing to the sum total of the grandeur that is Everest. Would I get caught in the secondary things in the Mahatma's character and magnify them and not see the sum total of the grandeur that is Gandhi? Many have done so. There is a book out entitled *What Does Gandhi Want?*, picking out the inconsistencies in his statements during the years. It is a microscopic examination, thoroughly done, but in the end the real man is lost. After you have looked at him through a miscroscope, you have to look at him through a telescope to get the total man. For he stands against a background of the ages and must be interpreted with that background to get the full stature and meaning of the man.

Many get caught in subsidiary statements and miss the sum total of the meaning of his teaching. A prominent man from the West has fastened on two statements made by Gandhi in *Young India*: "Its [Hinduism's] worship of the cow is, in my opinion, its unique contribution to the evolution of humanitarianism. Finally the discovery of the law of varnashrama [caste system] is a magnificent result of the ceaseless search for truth." "There," says this critic, "Mahatma Gandhi has picked out cow worship and caste as the unique contributions of Hinduism. What shall we think of a man like that?" And yet when you look at the Mahatma through the years, you see that it is not the worship of the cow but

5

6

the worship of God that has gripped him, molded him, and made him. He says that "the cow is a poem of pity," and "to protect her stands for the protection of the whole dumb creation." Thus interpreted it turns out to be different from cow worship. He says so: "The present ideas of cow worship and varnashrama are a caricature of what in my opinion the originals are." As for caste he so explains it that he explains it away; and in his life he breaks all the rules of caste, transcends them, adopts an outcaste as his daughter, and in the end does more to break down the system of caste than any other man, living or dead. In the Mahatma caste just didn't operate, no matter what he said about it. He was a man outgrowing constantly the literal interpretation of his words. He reconciled and transcended inconsistencies in himself. Would I get caught in the marginal and miss the central? That made me hesitate.

I hesitated for another reason. I have been intimately associated during forty years with the dual struggle taking place in India. There has been a struggle with the West in two phases: political and religious. India wanted political freedom—the right to make her own mistakes and to shape her own destiny. And then she wanted her soul to be her own, not dominated and molded by a seemingly foreign faith. There were many things in Hinduism which were unsatisfactory to modern Hindu minds, but at least it belonged to India, and they would defend it as such. They have defended it—the good and bad. Mahatma Gandhi was the spearhead of that political-religious battle. He was the voice.

I found myself very early taking sides with him in the political struggle. For years I was discreet—discreet enough to be able to stay in India during the years of struggle for independence. I went to Sir James Crerar, the Home Member, the head of the police of India, at the height of the struggle and told him my position: "I believe in the moral right of India to independence and am sympathetic toward the national leaders and their aims, but I give you my word of honor that I am not taking part in politics as such." I was allowed to stay. But later when the war came on, I felt I should throw aside a cramping discretion and expose my heart. I did so in many addresses in the West. For this I was refused a visa when I wanted to return to India in 1944. When I applied for a visa, I said: "I give my word of honor that I will not take part in politics, but I want the right, when asked, to say that I believe in the moral right of India to self-government. Would I be allowed that freedom?" It was a privilege to be kept out of India on that issue. I believed fundamentally in the method and motive of the struggle for political independence.

But the religious struggle with the West came home even closer to me. I was an evangelist in the midst of an India fighting with all her resources for freedom. What I presented seemed to be bound up with Western domination—the religious side of imperialism. I tried to present a disentangled Christ standing in his own right, apart from any mediation through the West. I tried to say that we of East and West stood in the same deep need—of him. My present plan of dividing my time equally between India and America—six months in each—is a practical application of my belief in our common need. I look on them both as mission fields. But no matter how much we tried to clarify our position and present a disentangled Christ, the clash was there. And Mahatma Gandhi voiced the protest. The pages of *Young India* were the debating ground. Other papers echoed the Mahatma and re-enforced his arguments and protests with their own. In my public meetings at question time these things would come to the surface, sometimes in bitter form. The center of that clash was this: since there was communal representation in India—representation in government according to the numbers in the religious community—religious conversion could be used to build up one's own communal power and incidentally to undermine the political power of the other community, which meant that the political power of the Hindus was jeopardized by conversions, especially mass conversions. For thirty years I lived at the nerve center of that clash. It has left scars on me. Again and again I found myself disagreeing with the Mahatma in his positions. For ten days he and I opened our hearts to each other in the early morning hours at the Sabarmati Ashram. There were deep disagreements. And yet something held me to him amid those disagreements. I felt that he had a way of coming out on the right side of things, even when the intellectual processes by which he arrived at that end could not be followed by me. He had a way of being right even when I thought he was wrong. His spirit transcended the mental processes and came out on the right side of things.

Acharya Kripalani, then president of the Indian National Congress, put it this way to me one day: "The Mahatma is more right when he is wrong than we are when we are right." That was a deep insight and is the key to the understanding of his character. His spirit and magnificent intention carried him past mental detours and brought him almost unerringly to his goal. His spirit was so great that it could absorb mental limitations and make something great even out of them. Many of us are correct in our little correctnesses and are small in the process. But the Mahatma was incorrect in many things and yet correct in the sum total—and big in the very inconsistencies. In the end he seldom or never came out at the wrong place. The words of Browning:

> I shall arrive! what time, what circuit first,
> I ask not: . . .
>
> . . . .
> In some time, [God's] good time, I shall arrive.

could be applied to Mahatma Gandhi in full measure.

And yet the above must be corrected, for it may leave the impression that he had a large capacity for blunders in thinking. That would be wrong. For he had an amazingly clear mind and an amazingly clear style and vocabulary. They were the expression of his inner spirit. He thought clearly because his intentions were simple and clear. He was not intellectually brilliant, but he was so fundamentally straight that his moral intentions carried him almost by intuition to right conclusions.

As I thought on all these things, I found myself coming to the conclusion that I could lay an honest tribute at the feet of the great little man. And could do it with my whole heart. To have won an evangelist to a whole-hearted affection amid the clash of thirty years is no small conquest. But in the end he had conquered me. This book is a sign of that conquest. Mahatma Gandhi wrote in the *Harijan* in 1938:

Intellectually, of course, even many people of the West have come to recognize the futility of violence, and have begun to ask if nonviolence may not after all be worth a trial. Dr. Stanley Jones has sent me a copy of his recent article, *Gandhian Solution of the Chinese Trouble*, and he has seriously discussed various forms of non-co-operation that may be successfully adopted. There was a time when Dr. Jones had not much belief in non-co-operation, but he now seriously suggests it as a nonviolent solution and has pressed me to go to Europe to preach peace.

"Had not much belief"—that expresses the distance I had to travel to where I am today. In the beginning I had none. But gradually the facts conquered me. If there are scars on my spirit, they are now radiant scars, for in the end I see something bigger than hurt from clashes. I see a man with whom I have often disagreed, but whom I have intensely believed in and loved, and I would like my readers to see the man I see. For Mahatma Gandhi has significance—very great significance, world significance in fact.

I am still an evangelist. I bow to Mahatma Gandhi, but I kneel at the feet of Christ and give him my full and final allegiance. And yet a little man, who fought a system in the framework of which I stand, has taught me more of the spirit of Christ than perhaps any other man in East or West. This book is a symbol of my gratitude.

And yet none of the things mentioned above could have overcome my hesitancy in writing this book had not the inner urge, which to me is an Inner Voice, said, "You must." Perhaps the years have prepared me to write this book.

E. STANLEY JONES

Contents

Preface

F EW people have presented as clear an interpretation of the spirit and leadership style of Mahatma Gandhi as did Dr. E. Stanley Jones, an American Christian missionary in India for over forty years. Dr. Jones knew Gandhi in a unique and personal way. *Gandhi: Portrayal of a Friend*, first published in 1948 (as *Mahatma Gandhi: An Interpretation*), contains quotations from letters and conversations between them.

This book reappears at a crucial time in our history. It is remarkably synchronistic that it can be read as a companion to the 1983 movie on Gandhi's life. In these pages, we are confronted with much more than Gandhi the person; we are brought face to face with the reality of our own choices for survival. For we are also a people who are being prepared to ponder our future as a nation and world. What alternatives remain for us as we reflect on violence, militaristic mind-sets, nuclear war, and world peace?

We Americans need clear guidelines through these anxiety-riddled days ahead. We need spiritual and social options and values which point us to Christ-like alternatives for personal and social change. We have a choice; are we going to continue tightening the boundary lines, constricting our options toward a global battleground? Or are we going to construct deliberate and courageous lines of humble nonviolent integrity? Dr. Jones' interpretation of Gandhi is a prophetic and timely guide to this end.

The Christ who affirms culture calls us to the cross through the example and influence of Gandhi. It is time that we take up our nonviolent crosses and follow Jesus during peacetime and at all times.

Hal Edwards, executive director
Christian Laity of Chicago
May 1983

CHAPTER I

The End of the Road

ON the day that Mahatma Gandhi was killed, I arrived in Delhi just an hour and a quarter before the tragedy. I had requested a friend to get me an appointment with Mahatma Gandhi for that afternoon. But my train was five hours late—symbol of India's internal upset—and when I arrived I was told that the appointment could not be arranged as he was taking a minimum of interviews since his fast. It was then suggested that we go to the prayer meeting which he held daily and which would possibly give an opportunity for a word at the close. I had often seen him in the postprayer periods.

We had just time to make it and get back to a supper meeting at which I was to speak, along with the wife of Acharya Kripalani, the president of the Indian National Congress. We had time to make it, provided we took a taxi. That decided me against it, for the taxi would have to wait and that would be expensive. I allowed the expense item to decide the matter. I said to my friend that I could see Gandhi later on my return to Delhi for a series of lectures, but the real reason was the expense. I am ashamed to confess that a matter of rupees kept me from being at the greatest tragedy since the Son of God died on a cross. In a way I am grateful I was spared the sight, but one would like to have been near him in his last moments.

I was walking up and down near the Y.M.C.A. building thinking of what I was going to say in the coming supper meeting, when the playing in the field alongside stopped as if by a silent, but imperious command. An awful hush settled on everything. This was a symbol of what had taken place all over Delhi and India. What had happened? One of the players ran over to me and broke the news—the Mahatma had been shot and killed on his way to the prayer meeting! It was unbelievable. People stood in little clumps and discussed the tragedy. "Now," said a prominent man, "India is in for chaos. With the restraining influence of Mahatma Gandhi gone, India will sink into chaos." I quietly disagreed. I said that I thought Mahatma Gandhi would be greater in death than he had been in life, that

11

through this tragedy good would come to India. I didn't see just how, but I felt it would. I could not help thinking of the Cross and what happened through that tragedy. That tragedy-triumph held me inwardly steady.

We went over to the Congress House, where Acharya Kripalani lived, to get some firsthand word. He had gone to the side of the fallen leader. When we arrived, a big Sikh guard saluted and said, "*Jai Hind*" (Victory to India). Was that a prophecy? Would victory come out of this to India? We went back and sat around the radio to hear Jawaharlal Nehru and Sardar Vallabhai Patel break the news to the nation. These strong men, veterans of many battles for independence—men who had gone to jail time after time without a quiver—now shook with emotion. They could scarcely go on, and their words were often unintelligible. Strong men in uniform sat by the radio and sobbed unashamedly. My tears mingled with theirs. Ours was a common sorrow. They asked me to read a passage and pray. I wondered if I could do it. An Englishman handed me the Apocrypha, and I read:

But the souls of the righteous are in the hand of God.

.   .   .   .

In the eyes of the foolish they seemed to have died;
And their departure was accounted to be their hurt,
And their journeying away from us to be their ruin:
But they are in peace.
For even if in the sight of men they be punished,
Their hope is full of immortality;
And having borne a little chastening, they shall receive great good;
Because God made trial of them, and found them worthy of himself.
As gold in the furnace he proved them,
And as a whole burnt offering he accepted them.
And in the time of their visitation they shall shine forth,
And as sparks among stubble they shall run to and fro.
They shall judge nations, and have dominion over peoples.

—Wisdom of Solomon 3:1-8

Every word seemed to apply to the Mahatma. I felt that in his martyrdom he would "judge nations" and would "have dominion over peoples." That has happened in a way of which I never dreamed. I prayed for a stricken nation—a broken prayer. An Indian commented as we ceased praying: "And this is Friday, too."

We called up Dr. John Matthai, the minister for transport, and suggested that we as Christians should pay our respects. He replied that he had tried to get to the Birla House, where the Mahatma lay, but could not get near because of the crowd. Three of us—British, Indian, American—walked the three miles to get a sight of him. We managed to get inside the gate; strangely enough, our white faces helped. We were told by a secretary that they were sorry but no one could see him till morning. We departed about midnight, not to sleep, but to meditate on the meaning of the tragedy of the day. For we knew that something of world significance had happened—something that men will talk about ten thousand years from now.

I wanted to see him that day to renew my plea for a national pageant which would be a befitting celebration, I thought, of the meaning of the nonviolent struggle for independence. Mahatma Gandhi had left the Ashram at Sabarmati on March 12, 1930, to go on "the Salt March." He proposed to march to the sea, 150 miles distant, to Dandi, and there make salt, which was a government monopoly, and thus civilly break the Salt Law and precipitate a crisis and go to jail, to be followed by tens of thousands of others. It was a dramatic launching of a Nonviolent Civil Disobedience Movement. It was made more dramatic by the announcement as he left that he would not return to the Ashram until he had gained independence for India. It seemed completely absurd. Here was a man in a loincloth and with a lathee (bamboo walking stick) going out to do battle with the greatest empire that ever existed and promising not to return until independence had been gained. Never were two sides more unequally matched. But here was something more than a little man and a stick. Here was the embodiment of an idea: he would match his capacity to suffer against the others' capacity to inflict the suffering, his soul force against physical force; he would not hate, but he would not obey, and he would wear down all resistance by an infinite capacity to take it. Here was a technique that had been applied here and there in history, but never applied to a problem on the scale of nothing less than the freedom of one fifth of the human race. The stakes were immense, and the cards seemed all stacked against him. How could he win? But we soon began to see the immense power of an embodied idea. The British were baffled. This was illustrated when a burly Irish military officer said to me: "If they'd only fight with weapons we understand, we would show them something. But this . . ." And he shook his head helplessly. Gandhi was getting behind the military armor and striking at the heart and conscience, and a great nation was striking back, but wincing under the blows falling upon its inner spirit.

After a struggle of seventeen years from the time he left the Ashram the battle was over. The little man had won. Independence was conceded. Never in human history had such a battle been fought with such weapons and with such a victory. My suggestion was that, now that independence had been won, Mahatmaji should come back to the Ashram, reversing the Salt March. Let him begin, say five or ten miles out, and march back over the same road with the same stick (the stick is in the Ashram Museum at Sabarmati), and that humble but triumphal march back would be a national pageant which would concentrate the attention of India—and the world—on the method by which independence was gained—the method of nonviolence. It would be a landmark in the history of the world. A new type of power had been revealed and demonstrated—the power of soul. Millions would line that road, I suggested, and I would like to be among them. I further suggested, not too seriously, that Mr. Attlee might march back with him, symbol of mutual consent to the victory.

I shared this suggestion for a national pageant celebrating independence with Sardar Vallabhai Patel, outstanding cabinet minister and deputy prime minister. He is "the iron man," and is not supposed to get excited. But he became most enthusiastic and said: "It would be wonderful. I'd like to be there, for I was the first one arrested on the Salt March. If you can get the Mahatma to agree, I'll arrange it." I wrote to the Mahatma and said that I knew that he did not like pageantry, but this was different; it would sum up the meaning of a movement. Would he come back to Sabarmati, say on March 12, 1948, eighteen years after he set out? He replied that "the withdrawal of the British troops from India would be the greatest pageant conceivable," and moreover, "I don't know when I will be able to leave my present haunts." He was then in Behar, where the anti-Moslem riots had taken place, and was preaching to the people to restore the burned houses and the loot, and those who had taken part in the rioting should come forward and confess it and take the consequences—go to jail. He was preaching a corporate and individual repentance to his people. In his letter he had not turned down the suggestion for a pageant, nor had he accepted it. It gave me hope that he might accept it at a future date. I shared this idea with other national leaders, like Premier Kher of Bombay, who was enthusiastic and said he would make all the arrangements since it was in his province. This was nearly a year ago when I first raised the question of the pageant, and the day he was killed I wanted to renew my suggestion to him. I had written beforehand to Rajkumari Amrit Kaur, minister of health in the Central Government, a Christian who was his private secretary for a long time before being appointed minister. I knew she was the best one to present it to him. After his death she wrote me his response: "When I presented the suggestion to him, he smiled and said, 'I must do or die here in Delhi. Nothing else matters now.'" It was just before he undertook his fast. He had the feeling, doubtless, that the crisis had come and the battle of the new India had to be fought out in Delhi; for this capital city was drenched in bitterness and hate after the blood bath of riots. Delhi was filled with refugees, and each refugee had his tale of death and loss. So Delhi was the nerve center of anti-Moslem hate. The battle for the new India must be lost or won there. And Mahatma Gandhi unerringly tackled the problem at the very center. As we look back, we marvel that he put his finger on the center of the problem—Delhi. That was a rare insight indeed. His last battle was the greatest and the most important. So he gently pushed aside the suggestion of a pageant and tackled the grim business of changing the heart and atmosphere of a nation. He pushed it aside, and rightly, for the thing he was entering had the feel of a real battle upon it—the battle for a new India with a new spirit.

My suggestion for a pageant was surpassed and supplanted by a pageant that only God could have produced. Alongside of what has happened my suggestion was poor, pale, and colorless. For the pageant that ensued after the assassination of the Mahatma was perhaps the greatest pageant that mankind has ever witnessed. The assassin fired three shots into the breast of Mahatma Gandhi as he walked toward the platform to begin the prayer meeting. This meeting was called a prayer meeting, but in addition to prayer it was really the daily message of the Mahatma to the nation. Here he commented on intimate affairs of the nation and gave his advice on current happenings. The people of India and the world listened. During the French Revolution a leader said to the crowd as a saintly priest was about to address them: "Listen, men, for forty years of pure living are about to address you." India knew when the Mahatma spoke that forty years of pure living and sacrificial struggle were about to address them. They hung upon every word as upon an oracle. That fateful day they waited breathlessly as usual for him to come to the prayer meeting. He was coming, leaning on the shoulders of two of his relatives, granddaughters. A man stepped forward and folded his hands in salutation and said, "You are late today, Mahatmaji." And then whipping out a pistol he fired three shots point-blank into the breast of the Mahatma. He sought to stop the Mahatma and his ideas. Stop him?

He only succeeded in freeing the ideas and spirit of the Mahatma from his frail body and making them the possession of the human race. For an astonishing thing took place. I had suggested that he march into Sabarmati in a humble, but triumphal procession. Instead he marched into the soul of humanity in the most triumphal march that any man ever made since the death and resurrection of the Son of God. The Roman triumphal processions were tawdry compared to this. It was world-wide; it was all-embracing. Never before had such a flood of love and sympathy been poured out as was poured out on the death of this strange little man. People from every land—people whom we never suspected as being interested in the Mahatma and his ideas and methods—poured out their affection. Even Winston Churchill, who some years ago had protested against the sight of "a half-naked fakir" coming up the steps of the Viceregal Lodge "to confer on equal terms with the representatives of His Majesty's Government," sent his tribute. And Jinnah haltingly spoke of "the loss to the Hindu nation"—not to the Pakistan nation, but only "to the Hindu nation." He thus revealed himself in the process of paying a grudging tribute. The Mahatma judged men, even in death, by their attitudes toward him. Incidentally, let me say that a Moslem officer from Pakistan assured me that a great many in Pakistan expressed disappointment and disapproval of this grudging tribute of Jinnah. The prime minister of Pakistan referred to Mahatma Gandhi as "the father of us both." All Pakistan was plunged in mourning.

What was the secret of this little man? How can we interpret him and the world's interest in him? Why did he draw men even when they disagreed with him? Men came to see him with blood on their horns and came away subdued and captivated. Why? Why did his death shake the heart and conscience of the world? What is this power wrapped up in such a strange wrapping? Did humanity see in him something they have been looking for? He began life as a timid boy who used to run home from school lest the boys tease him or poke fun at him. This timid boy becomes one of the world's bravest men, defying social custom and confronting empires with unbreakable courage. How do we interpret him?

CHAPTER II

Antitheses Strongly Marked

A FRENCH philosopher once said that "no man is strong unless he bears within his character antitheses strongly marked." One of the secrets of Mahatma Gandhi's strength was just this holding in a living blend and balance strongly marked antitheses. He was a combination, a meeting place of currents. And yet he was no mere patchwork of qualities gathered from here and there. The ensemble was unique. In the end an entirely new thing emerged —the character of Mahatma Gandhi.

He was a combination of East and West. The soul of Mahatma Gandhi was intensely Eastern. Born in a native state, Porbandar, where his father was the prime minister, he early imbibed ideas of independence. He was Indian to the core, and yet he was deeply influenced by the West. Had Mahatma Gandhi not been educated in large measure in the West, he would never have had the world-wide influence he has had. He stepped out of India and exposed himself to the West, studied law in Britain. He even tried to absorb the civilization of the West—dinner clothes, spats, meat-eating, and all. But he soon saw that this wasn't for him. It was like Saul's armor on David. It didn't fit. A friend who is one of God's troubadours once said: "People give me their clothes, but they soon begin to look like me." The clothes and the person became a unit. But Gandhi never really inwardly surrendered to Western civilization. He had his inner reservation, so the clothes never really fitted him. They were discarded.

Just as David, when they put Saul's armor on him, laid it aside and took the pebbles from his own brook, so the Mahatma laid aside the social armor of the West and took the simple pebbles out of his own national brook. To change the figure, he would plant his receiving posts deep in the soil of his own culture, and then he could lift his antennae to receive from the rest of the world—then and then only. It was a wise decision. In Gandhi you see a truly Indian soul flowering, and yet he absorbed much from the West and was at home in its language and literature. His use of English was remarkable for its clarity and correctness. I have never seen him make a mistake in English. It was not ornate, for that would not have fitted the soul of Gandhi. His language was simple and direct as his soul was simple and direct.

It was a providence of God that he was educated in large measure outside India, and also a providence of God that he had his training in Satyagraha (soul force) outside India. Had he begun in India, he would have got tangled up in the very complex problems which India presents. His apprenticeship in trying out the possibilities of soul force was gained in a simpler situation. South Africa furnished the rehearsal for the real drama of India. There he clarified his ideas and perfected his technique on a small scale. He might have floundered had he tried India straight off. But with the experience of South Africa behind, and the victories won through the method of nonviolent civil resistance, when he stepped on the stage of India he had confidence of direction and assurance of power to move along that path.

The twenty-six years he spent outside India can be likened to the years Moses spent in the mountainous country of Midian, until the day when the voice came out of the burning bush telling him to go down and deliver the people from the land of bondage. Mahatma Gandhi heard a voice come out of the fire of the struggle for the rights of Indians in South Africa saying that he must go and deliver the people of India from their bondage. He obeyed, tremblingly, as did Moses. But the man and the hour were matched. India was ripe and ready for a man who could voice her incoherent cry, could embody all her aspirations, and could lead her out of her bondage. A man was being trained in the West who would break the stranglehold of the West over the East. He was further trained in technique in South Africa, the nerve center of the world's clash of color; and from that training he would come out and deliver the man of color from the dominance of the white man. South Africa produced, by her very attitudes, the embodied influence which would eventually smash those attitudes, first in India and then in the rest of the world, including South Africa. The paradox is that South Africa, bent on maintaining white supremacy, produced by that very fact a man who became the greatest force in modern history in breaking that supremacy.

But if God was preparing Gandhi, he was also preparing Britain for this hour. There came into power in Britain at the right moment a group of men who believed essentially in what Gandhi was fighting for, namely, freedom, and believed in it for all men everywhere. They saw that you could have democracy or empire, but not both. They were inherently incompatible. So these men proceeded to turn empire into commonwealth.

But wasn't Britain compelled to give freedom to India? Yes, in a way the hour of destiny had struck. The movement for freedom under Gandhi had become so overwhelming that nothing could stop it or stay it. Britain had reached the end of her capacity to help India. The Labor Party saw this and, further, found this historic situation fitting in with their own principles, so they determined to meet the situation with decisiveness and straightforwardness.

The situation in India in 1946 was ripe for revolution. It was as bitter as gall. You could squeeze the gall out of the atmosphere. And then came the speech of Attlee. They say he is no speaker, but he made a speech that will go down in history as one of the great speeches of all time. He said the four things India was waiting to hear: (1) India would have independence (the word used for the first time); (2) independence would be within or without the commonwealth, and India would decide; (3) if India decided to go out of the commonwealth, Britain would try to make the transition as smooth as possible; (4) no minority would hold back the progress of the majority. This was so clear, without weasel words, and so honest that it changed the emotional climate of a subcontinent overnight. It is seldom in the annals of human history that a speech of one man is able to change the attitude of a subcontinent, but Attlee's speech did just that. The reaction of an Indian judge the next day was interesting.

"That speech of Attlee made me sad," he said.

"Made you sad?" I asked. "Why, that was a great speech."

"Yes," he said, "it was. But when a man talks like that, I don't want him to go."

A few nights later I was at a dinner given by a Brahman to meet leading men of the city. I remarked at the close: "For the first time in forty years I find myself in a mixed gathering of this kind, made up of men of the East and West, without any sense of tension. Something has happened. This reminds me more of what we Christians call a sacrament, a sacramental meal, rather than just a dinner." East and West were drawing together. Some strange force was binding us.

While the British Cabinet Mission was in India, I spoke in the Free Church in Delhi. One of the cabinet ministers read the lesson. They sang a hymn I had never heard sung in India before; in fact it could not have been sung before, not by a mixed audience such as this was, consisting of Indian civilians and British soldiers:

> These things shall be: a loftier race
> Than e'er the world hath known shall rise
> With flame of freedom in their souls
> And light of knowledge in their eyes.

And both sides sang it, and sang it from the heart, and both had now the "flame of freedom in their souls." I was moved to my depths, for I saw that Britain in conceding freedom to India was gaining freedom for herself. The inner conflicts and debates and apologies and defenses were over, and Britain was again with the flame of freedom in her own soul. She was becoming free in India's freedom. She was losing empire, but finding herself. The authentic voice of British democracy was speaking through the Labor leaders. Gandhi was giving a new freedom to Britain in gaining freedom for India. That is the uniqueness of his method and spirit.

Sri Prakasa, now High Commissioner to Pakistan, was at a tea party with a group of us in Benares during the struggle for freedom. He laughingly said: "I must eat as many of these sandwiches as possible, for I shall soon be on His Majesty's Government jail fare." He knew he would soon be in jail. And was. But he added this: "We can thank our lucky stars that we are fighting a people like the British, who have something in them to which we can appeal." A strange kind of warfare where you see the good in your opponent and appeal to it—and succeed! And then he added: "We will send out the British as masters; but before the boat has gone out of the harbor, we will call them back as friends." They have. The British are now popular in India. On the train a few weeks ago a group of Indians were talking in their corner; and as they were going out, one of them turned to me and said, "We've been praising you to the skies." They thought I was British! If the Indians were allowed, without political complications, to elect a governor general, they might elect Lord Mountbatten! He was at the bedside of the fallen leader, sat beside the funeral pyre, went with his ashes to Allahabad, where they were to be strewn in the waters at the junction of the Ganges and Jumna rivers. He has won the heart of India in an amazing way. In the independence celebrations he got almost as many cries of *"Ki jai!"* (Hail!) as the national leaders. Two nations were separating, and separating as friends. This seldom happens in human history. It is a miracle. But it has happened in India. Britain and India are being cemented together. And the hand of Gandhi laid the cement. He is the architect of the new India and is also the architect of new relations with Britain. To win your freedom from a nation and win that nation in the process is an achievement, and a great one. Apart from the method and spirit of Gandhi it could not have been done. It is true that some officials and businessmen have left India sullen and disgruntled, and they are spreading disaffection toward India in the West. But on the whole these two nations have parted as friends. I repeat, it is a miracle.

When the cabinet ministers were about to leave India after completing their work of marking out the steps to independence, I wrote them a letter thanking them for what they had done. I said that as an American I admired their spirit and patience, which I felt was a Christian patience; that their work would go down in history as one of the great achievements of all time. The secretary of the Cabinet Mission wrote back and said: "You will not misunderstand me when I say that if anything has been done, it has been by the grace of God, and by such help as you and others have so generously given, for which 'Thank you' and 'Thank you.'" Here were several new notes which revealed a new spirit in political affairs. One was that I, who had been kept out of India by the British government during the war because I believed in India's independence, was now being thanked by a secretary of that same government for helping—in however small a measure, for I was only working behind the scenes trying to reconcile—in attaining that independence. That was new. And second, the secretary recognized that their achievements were "by the grace of God," and he meant it. And they were. For as God had been preparing India through Gandhi, so he had been preparing Britain through the Labor Party to make it possible for East and West to meet on equal terms, be friends, and to work out their destinies together.

In the person of Mahatma Gandhi, East and West met; and through his methods and spirit they were in large measure reconciled.

Another set of contradictions was reconciled in Gandhi. He was an urban man who became identified with the peasant. His whole upbringing and training was to be a man of the city. As he was the son of a prime minister of a native state, his sympathies would thus tend to be with the ruling classes. But by deliberate intention he identified himself with the masses of the people, 75 per cent of whom are peasants. He put aside all superior clothes and wore only what the peasant wears, namely, a loincloth or dhoti. The upper portion of his body was bare in life; and when he was carried out to the funeral pyre, it was befittingly bare in death. And yet he always seemed completely clothed. In an elevator in America was this sign: "No one is fully clothed unless he wears a smile." Mahatma Gandhi was fully clothed, for he always wore a smile which drew attention to his face rather than to his bare body. His son Devadas Gandhi said of his father: "Gandhi was one of the most refined persons in the world, refined in his scanty dress, in his speech, and in his manners." Anyone who came into contact with Gandhi would verify that. He always went third-class while traveling, and third-class is hard wooden benches. In later years those who loved him saw that he must be protected from the crowds in third-class, so they sent him by special railway carriage or train, but it was third-class still.

An urban man becomes the idol and voice of the masses. The millions of India live in the rural sections of India, and it was Gandhi who aroused them, made them shed their fear, and made them conscious of destiny. Before the advent of Gandhi the nationalist movement was among the intellectuals. He carried it to the masses. Nobody else in history was acclaimed by such multitudes of humanity who everywhere thronged to get a sight of the Mahatma. They saw in him their best selves and their own possibilities. He was the voice of the dumb millions.

When he went to Delhi, he stayed at the Bhangi or Outcaste Colony—of all places! British cabinet ministers and viceroys would come to see Mahatma Gandhi at the Outcaste Colony. The multitudes—Brahmans and all—thronged to this Scavenger Settlement, a place unclean in itself, to get a glimpse of him and to hear him at the prayer meetings. For them he purified everything.

I was on the train one day, and the latrine of the compartment was very dirty, so I got a broom and cleaned it. The Indians in the compartment were amazed that I should do this, and one said, "You must have been with Mahatma Gandhi." When I said I had been and had learned this from him, they remarked, "That explains it."

When a delegation of Indians headed by an American missionary, representing a Graduates Association, called on Mahatma Gandhi and asked him what they could do to help the city, he answered in two words: "Become scavengers." He meant they should help clean up the city, physically, mentally, and morally.

But while Mahatma Gandhi usually lived in the Bhangi Colony at Delhi, when he was killed he was the guest of Birla, one of the richest industrialists of India. (The house was turned over to the nation, so the report ran. But this has since been contradicted, and Birla says he is keeping it as his personal possession. This is a mistake. It belongs to the nation as a national shrine; if not legally, then morally.) The Mahatma was equally at home with a Bhangi or a Birla. He fulfilled that verse where Paul says: "I have been initiated into the secret for all sorts and conditions of life, for plenty and for hunger, for prosperity and for privations" (Phil. 4:12 Moffatt). A man is weak if he can stand poverty only, or prosperity only. He is strong if he can take either one that comes and use it for the purposes for which he lives. Gandhi had been initiated into this secret.

In Mahatmaji the urban and the rural came together, not in an artificial amalgam, but in a living blend. He never patronized the poor; he was one of them, lived and spoke for them, was bone of their bone and pain of their pain. He was a man among men. The rich urban man and the poor peasant were both just men.

Again, we find in Mahatma Gandhi a coming together of the passive and the militant. The man who is only passive is weak, and the man who is only militant is weak; the strong man is both. He is passively militant and militantly passive. The Mahatma was both. He was always resisting something, and yet he did it passively; hence he called it passive resistance. But only if we understand the word "passive" in its original root form, "to suffer quietly, patiently." It was resisting, not by inflicting suffering, but by taking suffering on himself. It was really not a passive resistance; it was an active resistance from a higher level. The opponent strikes you on your cheek, and you strike him on the heart by your amazing spiritual audacity in turning the other cheek. You wrest the offensive from him by refusing to take his weapons, by keeping your own, and by striking him in his conscience from a higher level. He hits you physically, and you hit him spiritually.

The Mahatma was always resisting something; he fought on many fronts simultaneously—the political, the economic, the social, the religious. Analyze his fasts; they were against individuals, groups, communities, nations. He even fasted against himself for self-purification. Never did a man fight so long and continuously on so many issues. Nothing vital to India was alien to him. Wherever there was hurt, he inflicted on himself an answering hurt. His wounds answered their wounds. And yet he was no dour-faced tilter at every windmill he passed. He carefully chose his issues; and once convinced that a wrong was being done, he would inflict on himself pain until that wrong was righted. But amid it all he was cheerful. He was the Happy Warrior. He held together in a living blend the opposite qualities of passive and militant.

Again, he was an ascetic and a servant. The combination is a new phenomenon in India. The ascetic in general does not serve. His idea of the Ultimate precludes serving. For in the Vedantic philosophy, which is the central philosophy of India, the Ultimate Reality, Brahma, is nonserving. He, or It, is lifted above all action; for where there is action, there is the fruit of action; and where there is fruit of action, there is rebirth; and where there is rebirth, there is suffering. So Brahma is the actionless, passionless IT. In order to realize your unity with Brahma, it is necessary to reduce your contacts with the world of sense, sit and meditate and keep affirming your unity with Brahma—*Aham Brahmasmi*, I am Brahma. It is better then to do nothing, good or bad. The aim is not to do, but to realize. The whole attention of the ascetic is to get out of the wheel of existence. This whole weary round is maya, or illusion. The moral and material drain on a country, with hundreds of thousands of ascetics turning their attention away from the solution of problems to an escape from those problems, is enormous. It is true that bodies like Ramakrishna Mission are bodies of modern ascetics who serve and make a great contribution to the country's uplift. But the impulse to do this does not come out of the philosophic idea of Nirguna Brahma.

It was with a sigh of relief that India saw in her greatest son the combination of two things that gripped her deeply. India has always respected the man who could renounce, who could sit lightly to the things of this world. Buddha and his renunciation of a princely inheritance grip the soul of India. And here was Mahatma Gandhi, the leader of the new India, an ascetic. It gripped the soul of ancient India. But he also gripped the soul of modern India. For modern

India feels that to renounce and not to relate that renunciation to the needs around one is worse than useless; it is a drain. In the Mahatma the two came together—the old idea and the new—and were found to be in a living blend. Gandhiji was the ascetic who served. That drew both groups to him, for each saw its idea fulfilled in him. So the Mahatma was not merely a person; he was the meeting place of two streams, the old and the new.

Akin to this, the Mahatma combined the mystical and the practical. He was the mystic who arose at 4 A.M. for his morning devotions and who heard the Inner Voice in all the great crises of his life giving him direction. And yet that mysticism was intensely practical. The symbol of this was the fact that he would carry on religious exercises and discussions while spinning with his spinning wheel. That spinning wheel was the symbol of his identification with the poor of India. Their cottage industries had been ruined by the introduction of power machinery. Too many people were thrown back upon the land. For six months of the year the peasant had little or nothing to occupy his time. The Mahatma fastened on the charkha, the spinning wheel, as the thing which could fill in that blank space and provide a subsidiary occupation, give independence, and would stand for India's protest against the breaking up of India's cottage economy. From the Ashram at Sabarmati, where the Mahatma sat, talked, and spun with his wheel, one could see on the opposite bank of the river the smokestacks of forty huge cotton mills—now over one hundred—rise against the sky line. Compared to that mighty power, symbolized in the smokestacks, the Mahatma with his charkha seemed a pathetic figure, trying to sweep back the oncoming ocean with a broom. Would industrialization overwhelm him? Again the Mahatma, though wrong, was profoundly right. The future lies with industrialization. When I ask any group of Indians what are the five needs of this new India, and in what order of importance, they always include industrialization in the list, some of them at the top. India must take people off the land where they have small, uneconomic holdings and put them into industry. Instead of being the producer of raw materials which are sent to the West and then sent back to India as manufactured products, India must manufacture her own goods to supply her own needs. I repeat, the future lies with industrialization. And yet the experience of the West shows that industrialization can produce misery in crowded slum areas and be the festering place for most of our problems. This is growingly true of India, where the housing of the workers is the worst of the world. The crowded chawls where as many as ten or a dozen live in one room, sometimes in two shifts, are the by-product of a ruthless, selfish industrialization. The orgy of strikes and riots is a natural corollary. In the West where industrialization has taken place decentralization is seen as a necessity: take the factories into the countryside and set up smaller units under better living conditions. Mahatma Gandhi with his spinning wheel is a pull in that direction. It is a protest and a pull. The Mahatma sitting athwart the road to rapid and ruthless industrialization says to the oncoming greedy-for-profit hordes: "Thou shalt not create million-aires and misery, palaces and hovels, mass production and mass poverty. Decentralize and put much of this back into the home." There is something magnificent in this protest. The Mahatma and his spinning wheel will be the conscience of the industrial movement. His sad eyes will look upon the large profits, and money-mad men will know that these profits are made out of the blood of the poor. Those eyes tell them that. India is bound to be industrialized. The future lies with Jawaharlal Nehru, the socialist, in this matter and not with the Mahatma, for Nehru believes in the utilization of power machinery for social and economic ends. But the Mahatma and his charkha are going to be the conscience and corrective of that move-ment. It may be that he will help India to avoid the mistakes and consequent misery which came from the rapid industrialization of the West. But beyond that the movement of the Mahatma will rein-state and create cottage industries which can exist side by side with industrialization. Cottage industries stand in their own right, and Mahatma Gandhi was right in standing for them.

I was in the Tata Steel Works on a day when Hindus, from an ancient custom, worshiped the tools of their trade, out of gratitude perhaps for what the tools had brought them, namely, their liveli-hood. But now the garlands were placed, not on the hand tools which they had formerly owned, but upon the huge machines owned by the owner of the factory. They bowed and worshiped the garlanded machines. It was pathetic. I said to myself: "Poor fellows, you worship these machines which have little or no social purpose. They are in operation for profit. If and when more efficient laborsaving machines are necessary to gain more profits, then out you will go as useless to tramp the streets as unemployed. And you worship that!" I see no hope except that this gigantic power be harnessed to the collective good. Profit sharing in which the worker feels he is a part of the business would be a first step. The ultimate placing of this power in the hands of all for the good of all—in other words, the socialization of industry—seems to be the way out. And capitalism can save itself if it will begin with profit sharing, and then work out with labor an equitable plan of socialization.

Mahatma Gandhi with his overemphasis on the charkha as the answer to the economic needs of India was wrong, and yet he was profoundly right, for at the heart of his contention is a right—the centrality and independence of the worker. He was a mystic, and yet he was a practical mystic—and very often most practical when he seemed impractical. The little devotee of the spinning wheel may help to turn the wheels of industry, not toward mere profits, but toward the profit of all.

These opposites also came into a blend in the Mahatma: the simple and the shrewd. They were so blended in him that many people not understanding him called him a political charlatan, especially in the early days. They thought that this simplicity that embodied such uncanny shrewdness was an unreal cloak—how could one be so simple and yet have a way of coming out on top? But he was both; his simplicity of outlook gave him an uncanny insight into the heart of problems and situations.

This was illustrated in a delicate situation when the Sikhs got out of hand in Delhi and perpetrated unbelievable brutalities. Jawaharlal Nehru went to one of their camps; and when a huge Sikh arose and wildly said that it was the duty of every Sikh to kill four Moslems in revenge for what had happened in Pakistan, Jawaharlal Nehru lost his temper and had to be restrained from attacking him singlehandedly. He told his Gurkha guards to leave. They refused: "We have our orders from our general; we cannot obey you." Nehru had to leave with the situation no better. Then Gandhi came, and the big Sikh repeated the same threat. The Mahatma quietly said in reply: "I am sorry I cannot restrain you from this killing. If you are determined to carry it on, then you must go back to Pakistan, where you left your wives and children, and carry it on there. So I will go to Dr. John Matthai, minister for transport, and will ask him for special trains to carry you back to Pakistan, so you can carry on your killing there." And he started to walk away. The would-be killers, they who prided themselves on being "lions," were stung to the quick by his thrust at some of them who had left their wives and children in Pakistan, and were dismayed at the prospect of going back there. They fell at his feet and begged him not to send them back. He drew up a list of undertakings which they signed then and there. This quick-acting insight which the Mahatma displayed in this crisis gives in epitome the combination of his simplicity and shrewdness. The combination of saint and politician was the expression of his simplicity and shrewdness.

There was another pair of opposites that came to a living blend in the Mahatma: he was a Hindu who was deeply Christian. He was fundamentally a Hindu. The roots of his spiritual life were not in Christ; they were in the Bhagavad-Gita. And yet in spite of himself, and in spite of his constant protests against the Christian faith as represented in the missionary movement in India, he was more Christianized than most Christians. I shall take up later this whole question at length, but just now note that the Hindu sees in him the flowering of Hinduism, and the Christian sees in him an illustration of the spirit of Christ that inspires and shames him. This combination draws together people of varying viewpoints and makes them feel they have a common center. The Hindus pay their tribute to a Hindu who was deeply Christianized, and the Christians pay their tribute to a man, Christian in spirit, who was a Hindu. It is a strange combination, but a fact and a significant fact.

When I asked Devadas Gandhi what he considered his father's outstanding characteristic and contribution, he replied: "His candor and his courtesy." This is a combination rarely seen; the candid are not courteous, and the courteous are not candid. But Mahatma Gandhi was both, and he was both at one and the same time. He spoke exactly what he thought, and yet did it so gently and courteously that you loved it even when it was cutting across your own views. He was a most amazing blend of the candid and the courteous.

Note another combination: the serious and the playful. Seldom has a man been driven by more serious purposes. They weighed upon him night and day, for he was seldom or never without a crowd around him. They dumped into his lap everything—their complaints, their hopes, their troubles, their longings, their struggles, and their sins. The Indian often says to you when he comes with a request: "You are my Ma-Bap—my Mother-Father." Gandhiji was the mother-father to a whole subcontinent. It was a serious business to be looked upon to solve the troubles of one fifth of the human race. And yet amid it all he was cheerful and at times playful. Lord Curzon said of Bishop Lefroy: "He had the zeal of a crusader, the spirit of a boy, and the heart of a woman." Mahatma Gandhi had all three, especially the spirit of a boy. Each evening at Sabarmati he would take an evening walk toward the jail a mile away with a troop of children around him and some of us older ones trooping behind. He played a game with the children of seeing who could touch the jail gate first. And yet those of us who knew how events were shaping knew that he would soon be in that jail, or a similar one, as a prisoner. He made a joke of it! At evening prayers the little children would crawl all over him and hang about his neck while he was talking. It didn't seem to embarrass him the slightest, nor did it embarrass the rest of us, for he too seemed to be as simple as a child, and a child about his neck was as befitting as a beautiful ornament around the neck of a beautiful woman. They coincided. And yet he was a very wise child, for he was talking very profound things.

When I wrote to him that I had been at Sabarmati after an absence of twenty-five years and raised the question of his coming back to the Ashram in a national pageant, he wrote and reminded me that the thing I had missed most at the Ashram was a mirror (something I had forgotten!), and then went on and talked about the suggestion of the pageant and what he was doing in Behar, namely, calling a nation to repentance. Laughing over the absence of a mirror in the midst of that! But that mirror held a mirror to his spirit: he was serious, and he was playful. But that playfulness was the expression of the rhythm of his spirit; he was so adjusted and harmonious that everything was a play-spell to him. That is real mastery.

Another pair of opposites came to a combination and blend in the Mahatma: he was a combination of stubbornness and yieldingness. He was a man underneath whose gentle ways was an iron will. When once he had made up his mind, nothing could deflect him from the course mapped out. Again and again he would say on reaching a decision: "Please do not try to dissuade me. It is settled." He wanted to save his followers and himself from futile discussions. When he started fasts, there would be a flood of telegrams and letters asking him to desist and using every possible plea. But it was all a breaking of waves against a Gibraltar. He would never desist until he felt the purpose was accomplished. Jails could not bend or break him; he went straight as an arrow to his goal, the most stubborn of men.

And yet he was disconcertingly yielding when he saw reason to yield. He took the breath out of his followers when he called off the Non-co-operation Movement when twenty-one policemen were killed by a mob at Chauri Chaura, saying that his was "a Himalayan blunder." They felt he had let them and the movement down, for they had forsaken all to follow him and go to jail. But again the Mahatma was right. He called off the movement for the time being to discipline his forces and get them ready for a more purified advance that would send them forward. Had he not called off the movement temporarily, it would have degenerated into physical violence; and the moment that was done, that moment its appeal and power were gone. He knew when to yield and when to compromise. He was a very rare combination of stubbornness and yieldingness.

This leads me to give another combination in the Mahatma: he was a combination of poise and power. This is a rare combination. Those who seek poise usually do it by reducing contacts with the world. They keep the world out to keep poise within. And then there are those who exert power to change outer environment, and they rarely have poise. The Mahatma had both poise and power. He could be very, very stern. It was disconcerting the way he would rebuke those who seemed to him to be in the wrong. He was no man-pleaser. He did not try to win people by being pleasant to them for the sake of winning them. He could be as cutting as a surgeon's knife—and as healing. For he never cut for the sake of cutting, for the sake of getting the better of an argument. He cut only out of what he considered necessity. And yet he did it so gently that one did not realize till afterward how deeply he had cut. He spoke the truth, but always in love. And the love was a kind of general anesthetic that made the cutting painless.

In addition to this quality of speaking the truth in love, he had learned to be inwardly quiet amid a multitude. A cyclone has a center of calm amid a fierce whirl around that center. The Mahatma was that center of calm amid the cyclone of happenings in India during the last thirty years. But the power of the cyclone resides in that center of calm. Gandhiji was the center of calm and the center of power. He was seldom or never ruffled, never hurried, never stormy, and yet he generated movements that shook empires and that shook the whole social system amid which he lived. He was the terrible meek. And his calm was a terrible calm—terrible yet tender. He moved from conference to conference—conferences which had the destiny of millions bound up in them—but he was always calm and unruffled. His life was like a goldfish in a bowl—no privacy from the multitudes—

and yet he learned to live an inner life amid these turbulent surroundings.

There was another pair of opposites meeting in the Mahatma: humility and self-assertiveness. He took himself very seriously, so much so that a great many thought him pontifical. He was. For he had a detached sense of mission. He looked on himself as an instrument of God. One of Gandhiji's companions in jail, a revered teacher, begged of him to eat more food and be careful about his health, and the Mahatma replied: "I am taking good care of my body. I feel as responsible as a pregnant woman. God in his infinite mercy has chosen, it seems to me, that I be instrumental in bringing forth India's freedom. I, therefore, cannot afford to die as yet." A Congressman told me that, when the crowds were pressing him, he said to those around him: "You are coming and going. If something happens to this body of mine, it will be the country's loss, not mine. So if you want to help the country, give me fifteen minutes rest." His self-assertiveness came out of the fact that he felt he was an instrument of God to bring about the deliverance of his people. But his humility came out of the same fact of having a sense of mission. Personal considerations were relegated to the rear; nothing mattered except the chosen mission. So he could talk about himself as though he were talking about another person. His humility was born of a sense of consciousness of greatness of mission. There was a dignity in his humility. He spoke humbly and yet with an amazing sense of self-assurance.

But none of the above contrasts meeting in Gandhiji explain his greatness without this pair of opposites: he was the meeting place of a person and a cause. The person had the significance of the cause which he embodied. That cause was the cause of India's freedom. It came to embodiment in Mahatma Gandhi. As a person, taken just as a person, he was not particularly significant. Of him it could be said as it was said of Paul: "His bodily presence is weak, and his speech contemptible." He had no commanding presence such as we associate with greatness. Close-cropped hair, large ears, teeth gone in front, nothing but a short loincloth, a pair of rough sandals, sometimes a shawl around his shoulders in colder weather, and a very plain face surmounted by large horn-rimmed spectacles. Gandhiji's bodily presence was weak, and his speech was contemptible. He was no orator, never lifted his voice above the conversational when talking to a multitude, and there was no attempt at producing an effect. Then why did the multitudes hang on every word as upon an oracle?

It was because they knew that when he spoke the cause of India's freedom spoke. That cause looked out of his eyes, stretched forth its hands as he stretched forth his hands, and suffered as he suffered. He had the significance of the cause with which he was identified. People in the West—and East—often through the years would say to me: "Isn't Gandhi a spent force; hasn't he played out?" My invariable reply was: "How can he be played out? He represents a deathless cause—the cause of India's freedom. As long as he is identified with that cause and is the embodiment of that cause, he is deathless." The reason we as Americans look on Lincoln as the greatest American is we see in Lincoln the cause of democracy come to embodiment. Democracy looks out of his sad eyes, touches us with his rugged hands, and speaks in his voice. Lincoln has the significance of the cause with which he was identified—the cause of democracy. The word of democracy became flesh in him. In Gandhi the word of freedom became flesh. When he spoke, freedom spoke. Gandhi was India.

When Lord Halifax, then Lord Irwin, was viceroy of India, he asked me if I thought he ought to try to get Gandhi to go to the Round Table Conference, about to be held in London to determine the next steps toward India's freedom. My reply was: "If you don't get Gandhi, you haven't got India, for Gandhi is India."

"I agree," he replied, "but I can't go down to the jail and ask him what his terms are."

"No," I replied, "you can't. But you can say the thing that will get Gandhi, namely, that you and your government will stand for immediate dominion status at the coming Round Table Conference. That will get Gandhi."

"That would be very difficult," he replied, "for that would precipitate a crisis in Britain which might send this Labor government out of power and bring in the Conservatives, and, though the Conservative Party is my party, India will find it more difficult to deal with them than with the present Labor government."

I saw no hope of a settlement at the coming Round Table Conference this side of an out-and-out offer of dominion status. I suggested to Lord Halifax, "A wise radicalism now will be true conservatism then," and, "He who gives quickly gives ten times." Had that been acted on then, much suffering and misunderstanding would have been saved. But Empire was still in the saddle and was unwilling to dismount and come down off its high horse.

But note when Lord Halifax said, "I can't go down to the jail and ask him what his terms are," he said a significant thing: Gandhi in jail was dictating terms! Here was a ruler asking for terms, or hesitating to ask for terms, from his prisoner. It made you wonder who was ruler and who was prisoner! For the prisoner dictated terms. The Mahatma once remarked: "I get the best bargains from behind prison bars." The viceroy sensed that Gandhi in jail was India in jail and that the jailed was jailing the jailor. Here was a new power that was emerging—the power of an embodied cause and a willingness to suffer for that cause. Britain unceasingly knew that in dealing with Gandhi they were not dealing with a person only, but with a cause embodied in that person. They had to handle him gingerly and with caution, for they knew that 400,000,000 restless people looked out of his eyes and spoke as he spoke.

I have said that Gandhi was India, but that has to be corrected: Gandhi *is* India. It was no mere chance that his ashes were scattered in the 114 rivers of India. For he belonged to all India—was bone of its bone, blood of its blood, and is now ashes of its ashes. In Gandhi an ancient civilization, bound and clamped by cramping custom and mental and physical chains, came to renaissance, a new birth, and was free. When men saluted Gandhi, they saluted the new India.

Gandhiji seemed very simple, and yet he was very complex. He was a meeting place of East and West, and yet represented the soul of the East; he was an urban man who became the voice of the peasant masses; he was passive and militant, and both at one and the same time; he was the ascetic and the servant, aloof from and yet with the multitudes, and with them as their servant; he was the mystical and the practical come to embodiment, the man of prayer and the man of the spinning wheel and ten thousand other practical things connected with economic redemption; he combined the Hindu and the Christian in himself, a Hindu at the center of his allegiance and yet deeply Christianized; he was the simple and the shrewd, the candid and the courteous; he combined the serious and the playful, a man who could shake empires and could tickle a child beneath the chin and gain a laugh and a friend; he had poise, but not the poise of retreat and aloofness; he had power to change situations by a deep identification; he was strangely humble and strangely self-assertive; and last of all, and perhaps the most important of all, he was a person who embodied a cause—the cause of India's freedom.

This combination of qualities made the Mahatma strong. Without those opposite virtues, held in a living blend, with his great drive he would have been a fanatic. But he was not a fanatic. No fanatic plays with children, and children do not love a fanatic. He was a man in whom opposing virtues and interests were held in a living tension and reconciliation. In the South Sea Islands there is a flower, perhaps the largest flower in the world, but its odor taken by itself is putrid, and yet mingled with the scents of the jungle its odor is rather pleasant. Had these virtues and interests in Gandhi not been balanced by opposite virtues and interests, they would have tended to stink in the nostrils of the world, but blended they give a sense of fragrance. You cannot think of him without a sense of inner pleasure and gratitude. The incense that rises from the memory of his life is "a sweet savour." But while the savor is sweet, the preponderating impression he leaves is not sweetness, but strength.

CHAPTER III

The Meaning of His Death

WHEN the news of the Mahatma's assassination reached our unbelieving ears, a flood of rumors came with it: "It was a Moslem who did it;" "No, it was a Hindu refugee from Bannu embittered by his experiences." And thus the rumors raced with the news.

It was a mercy that no Moslem did it; for if one had, there would probably have been a terrible retaliation upon the forty million Moslems left in India who did not migrate to Pakistan. They would have been at the mercy of the overwhelming Hindu majority.

If the death had to come, it could not have been over a better issue. At first we thought it was the act of a madman; it was a mad act, and the man who did it could only have been a madman. But the fact is that it was a deliberately planned act by a group who had a deliberately planned purpose, for a planned end. They resented the attitudes and acts of Mahatma Gandhi, for he was bent on an India for all, including Moslems. He, with Jawaharlal Nehru and the rest of the Congress leaders, wanted an India for all, under a secular democratic state.

Jawaharlal Nehru had, a few weeks before, made an address in Aligarh Moslem University which was a very historic address—an address that pointed to the direction of events in the future. This university had been the nerve center of the Pakistan agitation. They had disbanded the university classes for three months to give the students and professors opportunity to spread Pakistan propaganda. It was at Aligarh that the slogan "Pakistan or perish" was coined. Pakistan was created with all its attendant bloodshed and upset and mass emigrations and dismemberment of India. The Indian leaders had a right to be bitter against Aligarh, for it must take a major share of the blame for what happened. Jawaharlal Nehru might have been bitter in his denunciation, for he has a temper, and here was an occasion. Instead of being small and retaliating, he was large-minded and forgiving. He outlined the kind of India that they intended to produce—a secular state with equal opportunities for all. The Hindus, being in a

35

majority, would naturally have large influence, but there would be no special privileges for any and no disabilities to any. Would the Moslems become a part of that state with no divided allegiance? If so, they would be welcomed in spite of all that had happened. It was great-hearted and statesmanlike. It reminded one of Lincoln with his "malice toward none, with charity for all" as he spoke to the defeated South. Jawaharlal Nehru was never greater than in this hour. Would the Moslems accept the proffered hand of friendship and throw themselves in with this new India? It was a breathless moment in the history of India. The flowers that rained upon Jawaharlal Nehru from the balcony and the sustained ovation he received gave the answer. Large-heartedness was met with large response. The Moslems saw that their intolerable position had a way out; they could yet become a part of the India they had dismembered. The position of the forty million Moslems left in India after partition was an impossible position. They were leaderless, looked on as alien since they had advocated Pakistan, and were now without influence. But the address of Jawaharlal Nehru opened a door. That address will go down in history as one of the great addresses of the world. A man who is an agnostic took a truly Christian attitude—the forgiveness of enemies.

This address coincided with the fast of Mahatma Gandhi at Delhi. In this fast the Mahatma raised two issues: disunity and dishonesty. Before he began the fast, he read a letter exposing the dishonesty and corruption among some of the Congress leaders. It was a very courageous thing to do—to expose to the public the dishonesty of some of the Congress leaders, people he had trained through the years. The second issue was this augmented bitterness and hate between the Moslems and the Hindus—augmented by the mass killings in which both sides were guilty. The Mahatma in his fast said in effect: "I cannot live unless you become honest and unless you become united."

I happened to be at Government House at Lucknow when Her Excellency Sarojini Naidu, now governor of the United Provinces, was sending a telegram to the Mahatma during his fast. I asked if I could send one too. In it I congratulated the Mahatma on the two issues chosen—disunity and dishonesty. They were great issues, and I thanked God for him and his insight in raising these two issues in his own frail body and fasting because of them. This would be a great purifying force in India and the world. I told Mrs. Naidu that I was "sad and glad over the fast—sad that he was suffering, but glad that he had the courage and goodness to undertake it." She replied:

"Drop out the 'sad' and tell the students at the university to whom you are now going to speak that you are glad that we have a man great enough to do this act of purification for us."

It was a great fast with great objectives. But all the objectives were seemingly in favor of the Moslems. He laid down eight conditions, one of which was the restoration of the 117 mosques in Delhi which the Hindus and Sikhs had turned into dwellings or temples after the mass slayings. All these conditions were in favor of the Moslems. Some Hindus laid bare their feelings to me about the matter: "Why didn't he fast against Pakistan, for Pakistan is the guilty party? Ours was retaliation. They began it all and are therefore responsible for what happened."

My reply was simple: "The Mahatma's strategy is correct. Suppose he had fasted against Pakistan. They would possibly have shrugged their shoulders and said: 'Let him die. What is that to us?' The Mahatma had to fast against his friends, against those who loved him and who would change their attitudes before they would see him die. If the Hindus and Sikhs change, then that in turn may change the Mohammedans. His strategy is sound."

After he had fasted for six days and he had come to a very weakened condition, so much so that the doctors said they could not be responsible for the results if the fast was continued, with Dr. Rajendra Parshad, "The Gandhi of Behar," as mediator, both sides signed an agreement to meet the conditions laid down by Mahatma Gandhi. When he was assured that the agreement would be implemented, the fast was called off. It was a great moment, for a great agreement had been arrived at in the nick of time—just in time to save the Mahatma's life. And to have arrived at that agreement was a great accomplishment, for the atmosphere of Delhi was as bitter as gall. I had come to Delhi a few days before the fast, and it was a city of gloom and grudges. The huge railway station was piled high with the boxes and bags and bedding of the refugees, camping night and day right there with no other place to go, for everything else was filled to overflowing with these sad-eyed and hollow-cheeked refugees from Pakistan, each with his tale of bitter grief. Nothing but a great moral force could cleanse this festering pool of hate. The fast wrought a miracle. People began to parade the streets crying: "Save the Mahatma;" "Down with communal strife;" "Hindus and Moslems are brothers." These same mobs had been crying the opposite a few weeks before, and the streets were running red with blood. To change all that was a miracle of the first order, and Mahatma Gandhi did it. The Moslems saw in a flash that he was their friend. This fast proved it. Their doubts were over; he was willing to die to get certain things restored to them. It was a high moral moment in the history of humanity. A little man reached out and took into his heart two sins of his country, dishonesty and disunity, and bore them in his own body on a bed of fasting. And the country responded and in a deeply penitent mood promised, through its representatives, that it would change according to the Mahatma's behests. This was signed around his bed. A passage was read from the Gita and the Koran; the hymn "When I Survey the Wondrous Cross" was sung; and a glass of orange juice was handed him by Maulana Abul Kalam Azad, a Moslem Congressman. It was a great moral moment. The spirit of the Mahatma had triumphed over the hate and revenge in the hearts of people. The country received the news with a sigh of relief and gratitude.

But not all. A group of people represented by the assassin resented all this. They resented the objects of the fast, all in favor of the Moslems; they resented the fact that the Moslems were being reinstated in India on terms of equality of opportunity. They should be suppressed or wiped out. There should be a Hindustan for the Hindus. The mutterings of this group had come to an angry roar in the falling of a bomb at the Mahatma's prayer meeting some days previously. Mahatma Gandhi himself had a premonition that he might be shot. On the twenty-eighth of January, two days before he was killed, Rajkumari Amrit Kaur, who gave me this firsthand account, asked this question: "Were there any 'noises' in your prayer meeting today, Bapu?"

"No. But does that question mean that you are worrying about me? If I am to die by the bullet of a madman, I must do so smiling. There must be no anger within me. God must be in my heart and on my lips. And you promise me one thing. Should such a thing happen, you are not to shed one tear."

Here was supreme poise awaiting calmly anything that might happen. He was never nobler than in this utterance.

The assassin is from Poona, the section of India from which Shivaji, the Hindu hero who conquered the Mohammedans, hailed. Shivaji makes the Maratha's blood flow faster as he thinks of Hindu ascendancy over the Moslem invaders. And it was Shivaji who—in self-defense, it is now claimed—extended his hand to the Moslem ruler and ripped open his bowels with "a tiger claw" concealed in his palm. The assassin of the Mahatma was the inheritor of the idea of a

Hindu ascendancy without any scruples as to how that ascendancy was to be maintained. A "tiger claw" could be used if it got you your end. His "tiger claw" was modernized into a pistol, and his extended hand was a salutation to the Mahatma with folded hands.

So Mahatma Gandhi and his ideas must be got out of the way. He was a danger and a threat. When the three bullets of the assassin were fired, two ideas met. The assassin's bullets said, "Some." Mahatma Gandhi said, "All." It was some versus all. It was the age-long struggle that takes place in every land—a struggle for the privileges of some versus equal opportunity for all. Every land struggles with that issue. In America we have had eight great crises over that word "all." Each nation struggles with it in some form. The thing that happened in Delhi was the echo of the scene of long ago:

So the chief priests and the Pharisees gathered the council, and said: "What are we to do? . . . If we let him go on thus, every one will believe in him, and the Romans will come and destroy both our holy place and our nation." But one of them, Caiaphas, who was high priest that year, said to them, "You know nothing at all; you do not understand that it is expedient for you that one man should die for the people, and not that the whole nation should perish." (John 11:47-50 Revised Standard Version.)

Thus the privileged, nationalistic leaders reasoned then, and thus the same group, in an Indian setting, must have reasoned now. The death of one man would save the nation. So the assassin must have dressed himself up in the invisible robes of a Hindu deliverer.

If Mahatma Gandhi had been privileged to choose the issue for which he would have died, he could not have chosen a better issue. It exactly sums up his life. It makes his life and his death all of a piece. He lived for an India for all, and he died for an India for all. It was a fitting climax. He died on the altar of "all." We have no excuse for the mad act; but since Gandhiji was an instrument of God in his life, so he continued to be an instrument of God in his death. God has used the tragedy to further the very things for which he lived. Jesus sensed this possibility before his death: "The Prince of this world is coming. He has no hold on me; his coming will only serve . . ." (John 14:30, 31 Moffatt). Here was evil unwittingly serving the good. Evil put Jesus on a cross and through that cross helps redeem the world. This also happened to Mahatma Gandhi. The assassin's bullets were meant to stop Mahatma Gandhi and his ideas.

They succeeded only in freeing those ideas and in making them the possession of the human race. The assassin shot Mahatma Gandhi into immortality. He is stronger in death than he was in life. Millions around the world are now interested in the Mahatma and his ideas —millions who would have given him only a passing glance had he not died for his ideas, a martyr for the things for which he lived. No other human being ever summed up better in his death the things for which he lived.

And no other human being ever did anything more effectual in destroying the cause he was trying to preserve than did Godse, the assassin. For the communalism for which he stood has received a blow as a reaction which will probably destroy it. Nothing could have hit communalism harder than did the death of Mahatma Gandhi. Now to be a communalist is treason to the dead Mahatma. The communalist organizations are voluntarily disbanding or are being liquidated by government order. The *Rashtriya Swayamseva Sangh*—National Service Organization, a militant body to make a Hindu India—has been declared unlawful; and the *Mahasabha*, to which the R.S.S. was allied, has declared the severance of political activities from its program, confining itself henceforth to the social and economic and religious. I can conceive of nothing that would have effected this change in so short a time except the death of Mahatma Gandhi. The greatest hindrance to a new India's coming into being—communalism—has received a mortal blow by this one act. To be a communalist now is out of step with the times, to be a back number, to be no patriot, and to be untrue to the father of the country.

There were really two reasons back of the killing of the Mahatma: his wanting an India for all, Moslems included; and his nonviolence. The group which Godse represents feel that in advocating nonviolence the Mahatma was emasculating the Hindus. So Godse would stop by violence the nonviolent. Result? The opposite of what he hoped. He succeeded in loosing the power of nonviolence and making it a world issue. Gandhi today has proved the power of nonviolence and has proved it at the time when violence seemed most triumphant, namely, at the time of killing him. Violence was execrated most when it was executed most.

On one of the times I saw the Mahatma recently he said in reply to my remarking he was looking fit, "Don't you know? I am going to live 125 years," and he said it with a gay laugh, so characteristic of him. But it was a higher plan of God that he should not live that long. Had he done so, the country would have lovingly put him on the shelf in his decaying years, and would have honored him, but would not have followed him. Now he dies at the height of his powers, and at the pinnacle of his influence, for he never stood higher and more triumphant than after his last two fasts, one in Calcutta and the other in Delhi. He wrought miracles through them, and his influence was at its peak, and that means a very high peak indeed— probably higher than any other man attained in his lifetime, for never in history did men revere another man as did the millions of India revere the Mahatma. But note: almost as many were won to an allegiance to him by his death as by his life. His death won millions of unconverted, confirmed the halfhearted, and set on fire the convinced. A very noble type of Sikh pulled me aside one day and said in awed tones, "I went to that prayer meeting in which the Mahatma was killed, interested in him and his teaching. I came away a disciple." The New Testament word for martyr is "witness"; then Mahatmaji's martyrdom was a witness, a mighty witness to what he lived for, and that witness won millions in India and elsewhere.

If martyrdom can be defined as a willing sacrifice, then Gandhi's death was a martyrdom. He refused to allow the people attending the prayer meeting to be searched, although a bomb had been thrown previously. He felt it would not be fitting for a prayer meeting. He was a martyr. Now his ideas and spirit and influence are fixed by a martyrdom. They cannot be explained away or questioned, as he died for what he lived for. Never did a death more fittingly crown a life, save only one—that of the Son of God. On the human level this was the greatest and most befitting climax: a man on the way to a prayer meeting where he would pray for himself and his people, and where he would give his daily counsel, dies a martyr for an India for all. That is a stage that could be set only by the overruling hand of God. Gandhiji's life and death were all of a piece; he lived a martyr, and he died a martyr. He died on the altar of "all," and will be remembered by all as long as there is an India and a humanity. Jawaharlal Nehru said in his broadcast to the nation the night of Gandhiji's death: "A thousand years from now men will be thinking and talking about this hour." They will be, and will be better for the thinking and talking about one who was undoubtedly the world's greatest man. For in life and in death he was the same—the servant of a cause, and that cause was an India for all.

CHAPTER IV

The Coming into Being of Pakistan

I WOULD gladly have eliminated this chapter, but the Mahatma asked me to publish the correspondence and the conversation which took place between Jinnah and myself just before the decision to divide the country into Pakistan and India. I refrained from doing it while he was alive, for reasons which will become plain as the story is told; but while I could disregard the advice of the living Mahatma, I cannot so easily brush aside him now that he is a martyr. He commands even more obedience in death than in life. But I must not saddle the Mahatma with the responsibility. I take it on myself.

Pakistan means "pak," holy, and "stan," place—a holy place, the holy place of Islam. I first heard the word and idea about twelve or fifteen years ago at the home of Sir Mohamad Iqbal, the famous Moslem poet and philospher of Lahore. A very influential group of Moslems was present, including the Prince of Morocco. As they unfolded Pakistan, I could scarcely believe my ears, so I asked them incredulously: "But you don't mean it, do you?" They assured me they did, and the years have confirmed it. It seemed so fantastic and fanatical to divide India on the basis of religion—to set up a Moslem state where the Moslems were in the majority. India was one; and Indians, in spite of surface differences, were down underneath one people. The country was geographically and economically one. It seemed to outrage everything within me to think of dividing the country in this way. And what about the forty million Moslems left in India after partition? What would they get out of Pakistan except disillusionment? They would be strangers in a foreign land—and hostages. In the words of Sir Mirza Ismail, a leading Moslem: "Pakistan has hurt the forty million Moslems in India more than it has hurt India." But to express one's doubts did little good. The idea and movement grew, led by the single-track purpose of M. A. Jinnah.

The Moslems said they were unwilling to be a minority in a land with a Hindu majority. They remembered that they were rulers of a large part of India when the British took over. They were the proud inheritors of Islamic destiny and ascendancy, and would not be ruled over by Hindus. Moreover, they were afraid that the Hindus would not found a democracy with equal opportunities for all. They had some basis for this fear—in the beginning. For with the coming of provincial self-government in 1937 a good many of the lower ranks of the Congressmen, represented by the Arya Samaj and the Mahasabha, did act as though the country was going to be organized for the Hindus. But this could not be laid at the door of the Congress leaders. It grew out of a misconception in the lower ranks and often out of inexperience. Mistakes were made, without the realization that they were going to have serious consequences. For instance, I think it was a mistake for Mahatma Gandhi to talk of the coming of Rama Raj, the kingdom of Rama. Rama was an ancient Hindu prince who was deified. His wife Sita has become the ideal for Indian womanhood. It was a mistake, with consequences which the Mahatma did not realize, to talk of the coming of a new order based on Rama Raj. I think he saw the necessity of having a social order as the goal of a renovated Hinduism, for Hinduism had no such conception as the Kingdom of God on earth. To a group of his followers, when asked what he meant by Rama Raj, he replied: "I do not mean the Rama Raj of Valmiki or Tulsi Das. I mean Gandhi Raj—the kind of order I am working for." To a Christian inquirer he said emphatically: "I mean by it exactly what you mean by the Kingdom of God." But that explanation never got as far as the name. The Mahatma is out to restore an ancient Hindu state, was the way it sounded to the Moslems; at least they interpreted it that way. It was a mistake to use it. It has brought controversy and has done more harm than good.

There was another mistake in using "Bande Mataram" as the national hymn during the struggle for independence. "Bande Mataram" means "Hail to the Motherland" and would have been not particularly unsuitable, though certain lines point to idolatry, had it not been taken from Bankim Chandra Chatterji's novel in which the members of a Hindu monastery used "Bande Mataram" as a slogan and battle cry in fighting off the Mohammedan conquerors. Not many Hindus knew its origin, and so used it innocently. But it didn't go well with the Moslems. To use Rama Raj and "Bande Mataram" was a mistake, but it was a mistake of inexperience. They did not see the consequences in the midst of a national struggle. Both will drop out now. Rama Raj has never caught fire in the minds of the people. It had no content. India is looking for a new order based on equalitarian principles. In the Draft Constitution of India the opening lines are these:

We, the people of India, having solemnly resolved to constitute India into a Sovereign Democratic Republic and to secure to all its citizens: Justice, social, economic, political; Liberty of thought, expression, belief, faith, and worship; Equality of status and of opportunity; and to promote among them all Fraternity assuring the dignity of the individual and the unity of the nation . . .

That is clear and full of content. India is now looking for a suitable national anthem which will express the aspirations of all, of whatever creed. None has, as yet, been chosen.

The tide of demand for Pakistan rose into almost a frenzy. It was pictured as a Promised Land to the Moslems where Islamic culture and religion would be safe and where the Shariat (Moslem law) would be the basis of the state. Those who opposed Pakistan were opposing Islam.

While the British Cabinet Mission was in India in 1946, I took a copy of a letter which I had written to Jinnah to Mahatma Gandhi for his reactions. In this letter I suggested that: (1) the Congress should concede Pakistan and proceed to implement it, by (a) having the India Constituent Assembly and Pakistan Constituent Assembly meet simultaneously to work out their respective constitutions, (b) by having them meet together to work out a federal union; (2) Pakistan and India would form a federal union under which Pakistan would work as a unit, a state.

Mahatma Gandhi read the letter carefully and dismissed it by saying, "The Congress will not accept this. Pakistan is sin." I agreed that I would rather see the country united, that it was unfortunate and wrong to have Pakistan, but you had to take what you had and make the best out of it you could, that God can even use "sin" as he did at the cross. The Mahatma replied, "I'm surprised that you, a man of God, would approve a thing which is sin." I tried to say that I didn't approve of it, but I would use it and rescue out of it a federal union, if I could. But the Mahatma was adamant, and I left with a sense of defeat. As we went away, my Indian colleague commented, "He succeeded in putting you in the wrong." As we were going out of the enclosure, the young men at the gate said as we passed through, "Sir, please quit India." It was the first and only time I ever had that said to me, and I remember what a shiver it sent to my toes as I heard it. It was a leftover from the "Quit India Movement."

Mahatma Gandhi was trying desperately to hold India together undivided, and his reaction to my proposal was a symptom of that. At that stage he was not ready to concede Pakistan. The reaction of C. Rajagopalachari to my suggestion outlined above was interesting: "We, the Congress, begin the other way: union and then Pakistan under the union. You are an evangelist, and you are used to gradual conversion, so you begin at Pakistan and go to ultimate union."

Then a year rolled by, and Pakistan agitation had caused such riots and great tensions that the Congress leaders began to feel hopeless of a settlement. I saw Jinnah in April, 1947, just before partition was decided on. He did not rise when I came into the room, but sat still and motioned me to a chair. The world must come to his feet was the attitude. I begged him to hold the country together. I said that though I was from the South in the United States, it would have been a tragedy if we had won the Civil War and the country had been divided. We are all glad now that we are one people. I suggested that just as Utah, with its different religious faith, was a unit under a federal union, so Pakistan could be a state under a federal union, keeping its own religion and culture intact. And just as Utah is influential in the federal government, so Pakistan could be influential in the federal union of India and help shape its policies. His reply: "How large is Utah? We are a hundred million." And then I made this suggestion: "If the Congress would concede Pakistan, would you say that you would be willing to enter a union with the rest of India?" He went off on a tirade against the Hindus and the Congress, and my heart sank; I felt we were getting nowhere. I had suggested that the division of the future would be between conservative and radical on an economic basis, and not between Hindus and Moslems on a religious basis; that the conservative Hindu, Moslem, Sikh, and Christian would be on one side, and the radical Hindu, Moslem, Sikh, and Christian on the other side; that this would be a good division, for some want to conserve values, and some want to apply them to larger areas; that between the pull back of the conservative and the pull ahead of the radical, we make progress in a middle direction. He then told me why the Hindu and Moslem could not co-operate economically.

"Do you know," he said, "that Mahatma Gandhi and I are living under a different set of laws—he under Hindu law and I under Islamic law? We cannot co-operate. For instance, if a Moslem dies, his property is divided according to Islamic law; he cannot make a will. The Hindu can make a will. If a Moslem businessman dies and some member of the family wants a settlement, the business is put up at auction, and a Hindu bids it in. So we are constantly losing out to the Hindus. We cannot co-operate."

Then he suddenly stopped, reached for a cigarette, and his manner changed. He softened and said, "If I may say so, your suggestion is childish. [He had to put me in my place before he would accept anything I said!] But if the Congress will concede Pakistan, then I will say that I will enter a union with the rest of India."

"And mean it?" I said, grasping his arm.

"Yes, and mean it," he replied.

Well, this was the news that India was waiting to hear! It took my breath away. I replied as I left: "I don't know what Congress' reaction will be to this, but I feel sure they will do it." We parted on this cordial note.

I sent a letter with this account of Jinnah's statement to the viceroy by a special messenger, saying I gave it for what it was worth. I took it to Acharya Kripalani, the president of the Congress, and his reaction was: "There is no trouble about the Congress conceding Pakistan. We are fed up. We will concede Pakistan either within the union or without the union. Will you please get Mr. Jinnah to give us this in writing."

I took it also to Vallabhai Patel and Jawaharlal Nehru. They were skeptical. "There is a catch in it somewhere," said Nehru, "but it may prove a basis of agreement."

Vallabhai Patel was more skeptical still: "What does he mean by entering a union with the rest of India? Does he mean a treaty between sovereign nations?"

I replied, "I don't know, but we talked federal union."

So I wrote Jinnah as follows: "One point I would like to clarify about our talk. When you said that, if the Congress would concede Pakistan, then you would be willing to enter a union with the rest of India, I take it that you meant federal union. Is that correct?" He wrote in reply completely reversing himself, saying that I had entirely misunderstood him.

I had to send this account of what had happened to the people in whose breasts I had raised hopes of a possible settlement without dividing India. I ended my letter: "You will have to come to your conclusions. I have come to mine." The reply of one national leader was direct: "I am not surprised at your letter. You will remember I predicted as much." Another national leader replied: "I am not surprised at your second letter. It but confirms our own experience."

What had happened? C. Rajagopalachari, now governor general of India, thought that I had misunderstood Jinnah, that "it is yet another case of hearing what you want to hear." My reply was: "It is easy to misunderstand another in a conversation and to hear what you want to hear, but you don't take hold of a man's arm and say, 'And mean it?' and he replies: 'And mean it'—that is too specific to be misunderstood." Then what had really happened? My interpretation is this: When Jinnah said this to me, he was in a high moment—a luminous moment—and he meant it when he said it to me. He really saw that holding Pakistan under a federal union was the way out for everybody. But when I asked him to write this, then it had to go through the hands of a secretary and thus out to the outside world. That would take him out of the role of the uncompromising advocate of Pakistan and put him into the role of one who was ready to come to an agreement with India. He felt he couldn't suddenly reverse roles, so he had to cancel out the whole episode by writing this letter, reversing everything. I didn't acknowledge at all that I had misunderstood him, but wrote in reply that I believed that the moment when he said that to me was a high, luminous moment and that I hoped he would be true to the Jinnah of that hour, that he could go down in history as the uniter of India and not the divider. To this last letter I received no reply. I have come to the conclusion that there are two Jinnahs—one the hard, unbending, legalistic, proud Jinnah and the other a man who is amenable, friendly, and wants to do the right thing. This second Jinnah came out at the very end of the conversation. But he soon pushed him back and smothered him.

Just before I saw Jinnah, I had seen Liaqat Ali Khan, now the premier of Pakistan, then finance minister of the interim government, and had made the same plea to him about the unity of India based on our experience in America. I said that life in the individual goes through three stages: dependence, the childhood stage; independence, the adolescent stage; interdependence, the adult or mature stage. So nations go through the same three stages: dependence, the stage of imperialism; independence, the stage of national freedom; interdependence, the stage when we come to world government—the mature stage. He replied that he believed "in a federal union of the world." To which I replied: "Then you and I are not far apart, for I also believe in a world federal union. If you believe in a world federal union, why not begin in India and have a federal union here?" "Yes," he replied, "but we must pass through the stage of independence first." He thanked me for what he called "my noble efforts" and "my noble sentiments." I came away with a feeling that he was far more reasonable and open-minded than Jinnah.

I can see only two tiny points of light in the darkness of those interviews, and even they may turn out to be illusions. But both Jinnah and Liaqat Ali Khan expressed the possibility of an ultimate union with India. Jinnah expressed it and then reversed it. But it was there, and in that moment I got a glimpse of something that may hold possibilities for the future. Liaqat Ali Khan expressed the possibility of a federal union, but they would have to go through the stage of independence first. These are very tiny rays of hope, and they may turn out to be wishful thinking and therefore an illusion. But then again they may be based on solid necessity. For these two peoples are not two nations but one nation; they belong together. For traditionally, culturally, ethnically, economically, and geographically they are one people.

I do not see how Pakistan can work unless it is under a federal union with India. Here are one unit on the extreme northwest and another unit in the extreme east and no corridor between them. They are separated by twelve hundred miles and a foreign nation. Custom barriers are going up along the boundary lines, and trade will be choked by them. Inside a federal union trade would be free and natural, and each would have a wide market for its products. Financially Pakistan is a problem rather than a possibility. She is now living on the 550,000,000 rupees which the fast of Mahatma Gandhi sent into her coffers. There will be economic pressure brought upon Pakistan from within to become one with India in a federal union.

Then there will be another pressure—and a big one—from the forty million Moslems living in India. This is a large unit, almost as large as the sixty million of Pakistan. They will stay within India, for their roots are here; and besides, they are not very welcome when they go to Pakistan. Many are returning to India from Pakistan disillusioned. In the trains leaving Hyderabad, Sind, for India, one third of the passengers will be Hindu refugees from Pakistan, and two thirds will be Moslems returning to India in disillusionment. Even Sir Mohamad Iqbal, from whom I first heard of Pakistan, told Edward Thompson later that "he had advocated Pakistan because of his position as president of the Moslem League session, but he felt sure that it would be injurious to India as a whole and to Moslems specially." [1] These Moslems within India are left in a deplorable plight by the establishment of Pakistan. Nearly all the Hindus and Sikhs of West Pakistan have come to India since the partition, but forty million Moslems are left in India. They are hostages, without a leader, and they have been alienated by their advocacy of Pakistan. On the trains in North India there is often a sign over a compartment, "Compartment reserved for minorities," with a military guard. The "minorities" mean no one but Moslems. That will probably soon fade out, and these reserved compartments will be abolished, but it is symbolic of what has happened. In establishing a national home for sixty million Pakistan Moslems they have rendered forty million other Moslems homeless. That is in itself a poor bargain. Of course it is not quite true that these forty million are homeless. They can have a national home by becoming one with India. They will do so. They will have to in order to survive. But as they do so, they will bring more and more pressure upon Pakistan to unite with India in a federal union. For if Pakistan united with India in a federal union, then these Moslems living in India would no longer be leaderless and without influence. They would have everything to gain by a federal union. Moreover, Pakistan itself would have everything to gain by a federal union, for then there would be no foreign country lying athwart her separated portions of Eastern and Western Pakistan; she would have a free market, and the larger natural resources of India would be open to her; moreover she would be a very influential part of an India which would represent one fifth of the human race—and a progressive and powerful India too.

Pakistan is attempting to found a state upon Moslem law, the Shariat. To try to found a twentieth-century state on a sixth-century set of theocratic laws means one of two things: either the people in growing will break the laws, or the laws will break the people. Islamic law is founded, not on principles, but on rules. You don't outgrow principles, but you do outgrow rules. "Islam either finds a

[1] Jawaharlal Nehru, The Discovery of India, p. 354.

desert, or makes one." And I fear it will make one out of Pakistan if it founds it on the Shariat, a sixth-century conception. Jawaha Nehru said in his Aligarh University convocation address: "To tempt a theocracy on a sixth-century conception is a throwback, a going against the stream of history."

Pakistan must abandon its attempt to set up a theocracy based on the Shariat and instead have a secular state with equal opportunities for all and no special privileges for any. And she must abandon a separatist mentality and come back into a federal union with India, both for her own salvation and the salvation of the forty million Moslems in India. Again, Mahatma Gandhi was right when he said that Pakistan is sin. For it has turned out to be sin—sin against the millions who have perished as a result of partition, sin against those who have been uprooted from their native soil and made to seek a new beginning in a strange land, sin against the unity of a land that belongs fundamentally together, sin against the forty million Moslems who followed the will-o'-the-wisp of Pakistan and have floundered in the mire of disillusionment over the results. Moreover, there is this moral wrong which is at the center of Pakistan. The Moslems, represented by the Moslem League, did little or nothing to gain freedom for India. It was the Indian National Congress, which included many nationalist Moslems, that won it after years of struggle. Then the league stepped in at the close of that struggle and demanded a large share—an unearned share—and called it Pakistan. I was shocked when Gandhiji first used the word "sin," but I see that he had a way of hitting on the right word to express a situation.

But that does not mean that Mahatma Gandhi did not care for Moslems. The proof of his affection for them is to be found in the Delhi fast, and in the fact that he died on the altar of their inclusion in India on the basis of equality. He saw that Pakistan was sin, conceived in distrust, born in fear, and nurtured in hate. Yet he had a deep compassion for the sinner. Just as he called the British system of imperialism "satanic," and yet he had nothing but affection for individual Englishmen, so he felt that Pakistan was a wrong, and yet loved Moslems, even when they were doing the wrong, and was willing to fast unto death for them.

Some day when the bitterness has died down, I believe that Moslems will agree that the Mahatma was right and will make atonement for the wrong of severing India by coming back into a federal union. Then the Mahatma will not have protested and died in vain.

CHAPTER V

Gandhi and the Christian Faith

M Y first contact with Mahatma Gandhi was the one which brought me the most unalloyed joy of all the contacts through the years. It was soon after his return from South Africa when he was just beginning to take up the threads of his work in India. There was no area of conflict such as developed between him and the missionaries in later years over mass conversions and the right and the propriety of conversion in general. Our relations had not been clouded by that controversy in my first meeting with the Mahatma. He was not on the defensive, and I was not on the offensive. It was simple and natural and unstrained.

I was giving addresses in St. Stephen's College, Delhi, and Principal Rudra said rather casually: "Mr. Gandhi [that was before he became Mahatma, "The Great-souled"] is upstairs. Would you like to see him?" This was all in great contrast with later years; for in later years the house would have been surrounded night and day with a curious crowd, and to get an interview with him would not have been easy, for people from all over the world would have been pressing him for interviews. But here I was being asked if I would like to see him! He was seated on a bed surrounded by papers, and he greeted me with an engaging and contagious smile. Without preliminaries I went straight to my question: "How can we make Christianity naturalized in India, not a foreign thing, identified with a foreign government and a foreign people, but a part of the national life of India and contributing its power to India's uplift? What would you, as one of the Hindu leaders of India, tell me, a Christian, to do in order to make this possible?"

He responded with great clarity and directness: "First, I would suggest that all of you Christians, missionaries and all, must begin to live more like Jesus Christ. Second, practice your religion without adulterating it or toning it down. Third, emphasize love and make it your working force, for love is central in Christianity. Fourth, study the non-Christian religions more sympathetically to find the good that

51

is within them, in order to have a more sympathetic approach to the people."

A few days later I quoted these four things to a British High Court judge, and he remarked: "That's genius. To pick out four things like that is genius." It was. For he put his finger unerringly on the four weak spots in our individual and collective lives. First of all, we were worshiping Christ more than following him. Jesus said, "If any man serve me, let him follow me." It is possible to serve Christ and not follow him—not follow him in Christlike living. The Mahatma need not have said anything more. The first item was quite enough! But he said a more remarkable thing in the second: "Practice your religion without adulterating it or toning it down." We don't reject it; we reduce it—reduce it to a creed to be believed, or an emotion to be felt, or an institution to which we are to belong, or to a ceremony or rite to be undergone—anything but a life to be lived! "We have inoculated the world with a mild form of Christianity so that it is now proof against the real thing."

There is this further to note: the greatest Hindu leader says, Your faith doesn't need to be changed; it doesn't need to be added to or subtracted from; it needs to be lived as it is. If the first part of the suggestion about practicing sends us to our knees in penitence, the second part will keep us there in gratitude that we have a faith which doesn't need to be changed, but only needs to be lived. Mahatma Gandhi's saying this doesn't make it so, but it is reassurance of the highest kind when he does say it, for he did not hesitate to put his finger on a wrong or a weakness. Here he deliberately says there is no wrong or weakness in the thing itself; the weakness or wrong is in our practice. Suppose he had been able to say the opposite: "You practice something which is inherently wrong." That would have been fatal. "Smite the shepherd, and the sheep shall be scattered." Smite Jesus with a legitimate criticism, and we, the sheep, will be scattered and will perish. But the center holds. There is no demand to change Jesus; the demand is to change ourselves to make us more like Jesus. When I go to India, I have to apologize for many things: for Western civilization, for it is only partly Christianized; for the Christian Church, for it too is only partly Christianized; for myself, for I am only a Christian-in-the-making. But when it comes to Jesus, there are no apologies on my lips, for there are none in my heart. He is our one perfect possession. All else needs to be modified. He alone needs no change. He needs to be followed implicitly.

Then Gandhi put his finger on a third necessity: "Emphasize love and make it your working force, for love is central in Christianity." Here he doesn't mean love as a sentiment, but as an organized working force. For he was thinking of the content of Satyagraha, his working principle of "truth force," the taking on yourself of suffering and never giving it. This is love as a way of life when it meets obstacles. It was a technique of working on the love basis in a world of this kind. So when he asked the Christians to make love their "working force," he meant they should adopt it as a total way of life— to make the Cross operative in the political and economic as well as in the religious. This is the deepest challenge that has ever come to the Christian world, for it means nothing less than abandoning the whole war system and adopting Satyagraha instead. That this was no mere whimsical appeal of an eccentric man is seen by the fact that the Mahatma himself adopted it as a way of life and led the greatest mass movement in history on that basis and won independence for 400,000,000 people. It worked, and worked marvelously, and he deliberately asked the Christians to adopt it. We shall see later the possibilities bound up in it. Note here that Gandhi asked us to organize love instead of organizing force, for he said that love force is stronger than physical force. And he demonstrated that it is.

Fourth, "Study the non-Christian religions more sympathetically to find the good that is within them in order to have a more sympathetic approach to the people." This hits home. For undoubtedly we Christians have approached the non-Christian religions not always with sympathetic insight to see the good, but with critical attitudes to find the bad. The mentality behind that was, if we found something good, then that was one reason why we should not come with the gospel. But that older mentality was in large measure replaced with one of appreciation, for we saw that Jesus "came not to destroy but to fulfill," so that every truth found anywhere was a truth that pointed to him who is the Truth. We could therefore rejoice in finding truth anywhere, knowing that it was God-implanted and would be God-fulfilled in Christ. We knew that Jesus was not the enemy of any truth, found anywhere, but would lovingly gather it up in himself and fulfill it. But the end would not be a patchwork of truths; it would be a new product. This would not be eclecticism or syncretism. "Eclecticisms pick and choose; syncretisms combine; but only life assimilates." The gospel is life, so like a plant it reaches down into the soil of every culture and takes out things which have an affinity to its own life and takes them up into its purposes and makes a new product out of them according to the laws of its own being. The end is neither eclecticism nor syncretism, but life assimilating. We can be sympathetic to truth found anywhere and be true to our own gospel. We would be untrue if we took unsympathetic attitudes. Again the Mahatma was calling us back to be true to our own gospel.

I wish we could leave the whole of the relationships of the Mahatma with Christianity at this point. It is so wholesome, so sincere, and so deeply needed by us. I am sorry to have to leave this period of simple, unstrained relationships and take up a period when we, the missionaries, who seemed to have a natural affinity with the Mahatma often found ourselves at cross purposes with him through many years. Yet I for one clung to him through these clouded years and loved and defended him even when I couldn't always follow his reasoning. Something held my heart even when my mind couldn't follow. As I look back, I see that much of the blame must fall on us as missionaries, and we could do well to take his criticisms to heart and mend our ways and attitudes. In fairness, however, I must say that many of these ways and attitudes have been mended and many of the issues have been washed out by events. But some of his criticisms are still valid.

The decision of the Mahatma not to be a Christian was arrived at in South Africa. A great deal of pressure from within and without was brought to bear on the Mahatma to become a Christian—some of it legitimate and natural, and some otherwise. He decided against it. He said: "For me salvation lay within Hinduism." It was not easy for him to decide to be a Christian in the race-heavy atmosphere of South Africa. How could he really see Christ through all this racialism? He did see Christ in C. F. Andrews, and rightly, for the Indians themselves called him "C. F. A."—Christ's Faithful Apostle. But when C. F. A. was to speak in a church in South Africa, Gandhi was not allowed to enter the church because, forsooth, the color of his skin was not white. Andrews tells of being on board ship and going over to the deck passengers and picking up and fondling an Indian baby. When he came back to the South African white passengers, there were clouds on their faces, and one of them said: "You know, that just isn't done." A South African Negro professor said to me bitterly: "The only hope I can see is that the white nations are arming, and they will blow themselves and their civilization to pieces, and then maybe our chance will come." That was the atmosphere in which the Mahatma was called on to make his decision. And mind you, all this racialism was often very deeply religious and held to in the name of religion. It was not enough to say Christ was different, was lifted above race, and loved man as man. True, but his followers made him the sponsor of white rule and white ascendancy. How could Gandhi see Christ through that? Racialism has many sins to bear, but perhaps its worst sin was the obscuring of Christ in an hour when one of the greatest souls born of woman was making his decision.

And then again, Mahatma Gandhi tells of his contact with a Christian family in South Africa who gave him a standing invitation to dinner every Sunday, and afterwards they all attended the Wesleyan Church. He describes it:

The service did not make a favorable impression on me. The sermons seemed to be uninspiring. The congregation did not strike me as being particularly religious. They were not an assembly of devout souls; they appeared rather to be worldly-minded people going to church for recreation and in conformity to custom. Here, at times, I would involuntarily doze. I was ashamed, but some of my neighbors, who were in no better case, lightened the shame. I could not go on long like this, and soon gave up attending the service.

Shades of John Wesley! A Wesleyan church drowsy and dull at a moment when one of the world's greatest men sat in the pews and was slowly making up his mind. The judgment on the church may not be fair, and yet the impression was made.

He tried going directly to the Bible. He said:

I read the book of Genesis, and the chapters that followed invariably sent me to sleep. . . . I disliked reading the book of Numbers. But the New Testament produced a different impression, especially the Sermon on the Mount, which went straight to my heart. . . . That renunciation was the highest form of religion appealed to me greatly. Tolstoy's *The Kingdom of God Is Within You* overwhelmed me. It left an abiding impression on me. Before the independent thinking, profound morality, and the truthfulness of this book, all the other books given me by Mr. Coates seemed to pale into insignificance.

Though Mahatma Gandhi never became a Christian, yet there has been a deep strain of Christian thought and attitude running through him and his life. He says:

Though I took a path my Christian friends had not intended for me, I have remained ever indebted to them for the religious quest they awakened in me. I shall always cherish the memory of their contact. The years that followed had more, not less of sweet contacts in store for me.[1]

He tells of a later contact in India with Kali Charan Banerjee, a great Indian Christian:

I found there was much in common between Mr. Banerjee and myself. His simplicity, his humility, his courage, his truthfulness, all these things I have all along admired. . . . Well, I am not going to engage you in giving a description of the little discussion we had between us. It was very good, very noble. I came away not sorry, not dejected, not disappointed, but I felt sad that even Mr. Banerjee could not convince me. This was my final deliberate striving to realize Christianity as it was presented to me. Today my position is that, though I admire much in Christianity, I am unable to identify myself with orthodox Christianity. My life has been full of external tragedies, and, if they have not left any visible and indelible effect on me, I owe it to the teaching of the Bhagavad-Gita.

The Gita would henceforth be the center of his loyalty and his devotion. But this sentence is a curious one and may explain a good deal: "I came away not sorry, not dejected, not disappointed, but I felt sad that even Mr. Banerjee could not convince me." "Not sorry, . . . but I felt sad." This apparent contradiction may be the little chink in the fence that lets us see into an apparent contradiction in his life: He was a Hindu by allegiance and a Christian by affinity. He was a Hindu who was deeply Christianized—more Christianized than most Christians. One Christian editor described him as "a natural Christian," quoting the statement of Tertullian, *Anima naturaliter Christiana*"—the soul is naturally Christian. But we must not try to claim him when he himself would probably repudiate that claim. He was a Hindu and belonged to Hinduism; but nevertheless, when we strip away all controversies between East and West, and religion and religion, we cannot help recognizing affinities he had with the faith in Christ.

He often reminds me of the parable of the man with two sons whom he told to go to work in his vineyard. The first one said, "I go, sir," and did not go. The second said, "I go not, sir," and afterwards he changed his mind and went. "Which of these," asked the Master, "did his father's will?" And the answer was the latter. We as Christians are very like the son who said, "I go, sir—I will be a Christian," but in fact we don't go, not fully. Gandhiji is very like the son who said, "I go not, sir," and afterward he went—went by manifesting a Christian spirit far beyond most of the rest of us.

Hinduism must claim him, and rightly so. It has been suggested, perhaps not too seriously, that Hinduism should be renamed Gandhism, this as a memorial to the Mahatma. But if Hinduism claims him, it will not be an inexpensive claim. Many things that pass by the name of Hinduism will have to go if Gandhi stays. For while he has been the occasion of a tremendous revival of Hinduism, nevertheless he has been a disruptive force within Hinduism. He has been and is cracking the system. Many of the orthodox see this and have been afraid of him in their heart of hearts, even while paying him lip service. Some of this disgruntled orthodoxy even came to the surface and dared distribute sweets at his death. For instance, no one has been a greater force in the breaking of caste than Mahatma Gandhi. Caste as a system is crumbling, and the Mahatma by his insistance on getting rid of untouchability was the greatest influence in causing it to crumble. For when untouchability goes, caste goes. It is not possible to get rid of one and hold the other. And yet for a while the Mahatma tried it.

I went to see him when he was in the Yeravda jail. Dr. Ambedkar was seated with him as he sat on a bed in the jail courtyard. It was at the time of Dr. Ambedkar's announcement that he was leaving Hinduism and would take the depressed classes with him. It was an important conference the Mahatma was having with the leader of the outcastes, but he suspended the conference, and Dr. Ambedkar listened in to our conversation. I suggested that there were two views of society: one a horizontal view (and here I held my fingers in a horizontal way) and the other a vertical (and here I held my fingers in a vertical way). The horizontal view of life views man equal before God and therefore equal before man. The vertical view puts men in different strata, one on top of the other. Caste does that. These are the four castes: Brahman, the priestly class; Kshatriya, the warrior class; Vaisya, the trading class; and Sudra, the serving class. Below these are the untouchables, the seventy million who have no standing within caste; they are the outcastes. Now you propose to wipe out the untouchables by moving them up one step and amalgamating them within caste. But the caste system is still intact; life is still vertically conceived. Dr. Ambedkar laughed outright, for I had evidently touched on the very thing at issue, only I had put it in a little different way.

The Mahatma replied, "I would also say that we must conceive of life as horizontal—all equal before God and man."

"Then," I said, "caste has gone along with untouchability."

"Yes," he slowly replied, "it has. But there are certain qualities which are carried over from a previous birth which make differences in function in this one." He defended a modified form of caste, and this is what is meant when, in an article entitled "Why I Am a Hindu," he said, "Finally, the discovery of the law of varnashrama [the caste system] is a magnificent result of the ceaseless search for truth." But in his interpretation to me it was reduced to a coming over of differences in quality of being from a previous birth. This cannot be identified with the present caste system, which is based on birth in a particular home. One is inherent, and the other is artificial. Gandhiji's explanation of caste is to explain it away. And that is exactly what he has done. His defense turns out to be offense. There is no doubt whatever that Mahatma Gandhi was and is the greatest single force in breaking down caste. In his presence caste simply does not operate. For he transcends all differences in his all-embracing love. If he defends it with his lips, his heart smashes it at that very moment. But he did not defend caste; he defended something quite different.

It was difficult to fit Mahatma Gandhi into a system, philosophical or religious. He broke the molds. For instance, the three great philosophical doctrines of Hinduism are karma, transmigration, and identification with the impersonal Brahma. And yet as I listened to the radio for two days after his death, as eulogy after eulogy was heaped upon him, I suddenly woke up to the fact that he was not fitting any one of these three basic concepts. Not once was it suggested that the law of karma was operative in Mahatmaji, that in his death he was reaping what he sowed. An orthodox Hindu once said to me, "Jesus must have been a terrible sinner in a previous birth, for he was such a terrible sufferer in this one." That, according to the strict law of karma, would be correct. But this was never suggested in the case of Mahatmaji. His suffering was not punitive, but vicarious. He died for the nation and its sins. But that points to the Cross rather than to karma.

Again, not once was it suggested that the Mahatma would now

come back in a rebirth and grow up as a child and be another personality. They didn't want him to come back in transmigration; they wanted him to come back now in spirit and guide them. I have not heard it suggested once that we must now look for a child as the reincarnated Mahatma. The idea just doesn't fit.

Nor have I heard it suggested that the Mahatma has now been merged into the impersonal Brahma. The fact is they do not want him to be lost in the ocean of impersonal Being. They want him to survive as a personal being, as Mahatma Gandhi; and they want him to come back in spirit and lead them. This cry was voiced in the eloquent tribute to the Mahatma by Mrs. Sarojini Naidu, the poetess and patriot and now governor of the United Provinces, when she said in a nationwide broadcast:

"Greater love hath no man than this, that a man lay down his life for his friends." But there is one thing greater, and that is that he should rise again after laying down his life. This is the third day. He must rise again. O Bapuji, come back from the dead and lead us. We do not want you to rest. We need you too much.

This was the broken cry of a broken heart, and it exactly expressed India's mood. The idea of the Mahatma merging into an impersonal Essence and being lost as Mahatma Gandhi just didn't fit. So it was never expressed.

Not one of the central philosophical ideas—karma, transmigration, or merging into the impersonal Brahma—did seem to fit the Mahatma or be operative. Perhaps it would not be fair to say that all the ideas that were operative were Christian ideas. But it would be fair to say that they were more Christian than Hindu. Orthodox Hinduism took over his body and burned it according to Hindu orthodoxy, but the ideas and concepts he represented seemed strangely Christian. And yet again it would not be orthodox Christianity. The Mahatma was a natural Christian rather than an orthodox one. And yet how shall I defend that distinction? I don't. I leave it undefended. But it is the nearest statement of the facts I know.

But I must be honest with myself and my readers, for I cannot leave it at that, as though that were all there is to be said. There were areas of uncertainty in Mahatma Gandhi's life which are not found in the ordinary sincere out-and-out Christian, just as there are areas of application of the Christian way in Mahatma Gandhi not found or often found in the Christian. If the Mahatma had something of active application of the Christian way to give to the Christian, I think the Christian has something to give in the way of an experience of God which the Mahatma seemed to lack. "I have not seen Him, neither do I know Him, but I have made the world's faith in God my own," said the Mahatma. That is dim and unsatisfactory. And the reason is obvious. The Mahatma was influenced and molded by Christian principles, particularly the Sermon on the Mount. But he never seemed to get to Christ as a person. I once wrote him a letter and poured out my heart in it about this very question.

You know my love for you and how I've tried to interpret you and your nonviolent movement to the West. But I am rather disappointed in one matter. I thought you had grasped the center of the Christian faith, but I'm afraid I must change my mind. I think you have grasped certain principles of the Christian faith which have molded you and have helped make you great—you have grasped the principles, but you have missed the Person. You said in Calcutta to the missionaries that you did not turn to the Sermon on the Mount for consolation, but to the Bhagavad-Gita. Nor do I turn to the Sermon on the Mount for consolation, but to this Person who embodies and illustrates the Sermon on the Mount, but he is much more. Here is where I think you are weakest in your grasp. May I suggest that you penetrate through the principles to the Person and then come back and tell us what you have found. I don't say this as a mere Christian propagandist. I say this because we need you and need the illustration you could give us if you really grasped the center, the Person.

He wrote back an immediate reply:

I appreciate the love underlying the letter and kind thought for my welfare, but my difficulty is of long standing. Other friends have pointed it out to me before now. I cannot grasp the position by the intellect; the heart must be touched. Saul became Paul, not by an intellectual effort, but by something touching his heart. All I can say is that my heart is absolutely open; I have no axes to grind; I want to find truth, to see God face to face. But there I stop. Do please come to the Ashram when you have the time.

This is a revealing letter. He saw that there was something more than he had realized. He was missing something, but that something could not be realized by an intellectual effort, but by a heart revelation.

He was missing that heart revelation because he had not come into vital contact with the Person, Christ. He had only touched the Person at second hand through the principles. It was at this place that the ordinary sincere devotee of Christ goes beyond the Mahatma. By the Christian's self-surrender and faith and obedience a living contact with Christ brings certainty and joy and release from past and present sin which make him bubble with gratitude, and which make him want to share Christ with everybody. It was this the Mahatma never quite grasped, and this was the place of a great deal of the misunderstanding with Christians, particularly regarding evangelizing. He could not understand why they should want to share their faith.

A great many people came to India and asked the Mahatma foolish questions. Among the most foolish questions ever asked him was this one: "What do you think of Stanley Jones?" The Mahatma replied: "He is a very earnest man, and a very sincere man, but he is too certain about religion and therefore lacks humility." From the Mahatma's standpoint he was right, for he looked on salvation as an attainment through disciplined effort. While I was at the Ashram at Sabarmati, we used to go aside at the end of the prayer period which began at 4 A.M., and he would tell me what religion meant to him in experience, and I would tell him what it meant to me. For ten days we looked into each other's hearts. One day he said, "If one is to find salvation, he must have as much patience as a man who sits by the seaside and with a straw picks up a single drop of water, transfers it, and thus empties the ocean." Salvation comes through one's strict, disciplined efforts, a rigid self-mastery. If one believes that salvation comes through one's own disciplined efforts, then of course he dares not speak of it. To speak of it would be indelicate and would lack humility, for it is his own.

But I looked on salvation, not as an attainment through one's efforts, but as an obtainment through grace. I came to Christ morally and spiritually bankrupt with nothing to offer except my bankruptcy. To my astonishment he took me, forgave me, and sent my happy soul singing its way down the years. By grace was I saved through faith and that not of myself; it was the gift of God. I could talk about that, for in doing so I was laying the tribute of my love and gratitude at the feet of Another. Not to talk about it would be indelicate and would lack humility, for it would thus seem to be my own. So from the Mahatma's standpoint he was right, and from my standpoint I was right. It was at this place that the Christians and the Mahatma never got together. They were talking two different languages and never understood each other. He was talking the language of attainment, of works; and they were talking the language of obtainment, of grace. It seemed to him presumption to talk about a conscious redemption now through the conscious power and presence of the Redeemer. For salvation through effort struggles and sighs, but salvation by grace surrenders and sings. You are never sure you have attained, but you are sure that you have obtained. I know that salvation by grace seems too cheap and easy, but it is not cheap; for when you take the gift, you belong forever to the Giver. He has you to your depths —and forever. And the moment you take the gift, you feel that you want to put your arms around the world and share this with everybody. This the Mahatma could never understand.

He constantly said to the Indian Christians and the missionaries: "Don't talk about it. The rose doesn't have to propagate its perfume. It just gives it forth, and people are drawn to it. Don't talk about it. Live it. And people will come to see the source of your power." There is something in the criticism of the Mahatma, and it must be listened to. For very, very often our evangelism has been verbal instead of vital —an evangelism of the lips instead of an evangelism of the life. The whole life has not spoken the message. Because we could say certain phrases, we thought we were preaching the gospel—but deep hasn't spoken to deep. It hasn't been self-verifying with the witness of the life corroborating the witness of the words. In penance for this we might very well impose silence upon our lips until our lives have caught up with their testimony. We must take very seriously the rose perfume emphasis as a corrective. But only as a corrective. For to swing the other way and say that we will have an evangelism of the life, but not of the lips, is just as one-sided and unnatural. Suppose Jesus had done that. Suppose he had taken the stand that he would live the gospel, but he would not preach it. How much poorer the world would have been. We would have commemorated a beautiful life, but we would have had no gospel to communicate. But there was no hiatus between Jesus' words and his deeds; you can't tell where his words end and his deeds begin, for his deeds were words, and his words were deeds and, coming together with what he was, became the Word made flesh. It was all of a piece. To impose an unnatural silence on him would have been to bisect life, for our words are a part of our lives. "Out of the abundance of the heart the mouth speaketh." Besides, the perfume of the rose is the voice of the rose—the only voice it has—calling the bees to the nectar.

But the objection of the Mahatma to evangelism was more fundamental. He held that all religions are equal, and therefore to try to convert from one to another is wrong. An article written from the Yeravda jail was entitled "Tolerance, i.e., Equality of Religions." His tolerance was based on his conception of the equality of religions. He modified this in the article to "the equality of the principal faiths of the world." In other places he said, "All the great religions are equal." He put in "principal" and "great" to get over the difficulty of having to include animism and the lower forms of religion. But the moment he did that, he gave away his case, for he introduced a distinction. Some are equal, and some are not equal. Only the "principal" and "great" religions are equal. If this distinction holds at one level, why shouldn't it hold all the way through—some may be bad; some may be good and bad; some may be good; some may be better; and some may be best? Are we mentally to abdicate when it comes to the deepest choices of life? To take that attitude would stop all progress in every realm. Suppose at the time of the Ptolemaic and Copernican conflict the attitude had been taken: all great scientific theories are equal. That would have saved a controversy, but it would have killed progress, for one theory fitted the facts better and survived. The same with religions; some fit the facts better and will survive. The rest will be quietly laid aside as outworn.

But as I write this, I find myself with a deep hesitancy. I dislike exceedingly to feel that one must enter what may turn out to be an unholy rivalry. For I do not conceive of the gospel of Christ as a religion at all. Jesus never used the word. It was foreign to his conception. He was not coming to set one religion over against another. He came to set the gospel over against human need, whether that need be in the Jewish faith, the Gentile religions, or among Jesus' own followers. "There are many religions; there is but one gospel." For religions are man's search for God; the gospel is God's search for man. One is from man up to God, and the other is from God down to man.

I know, when I say that, it sounds presumptuous, for a religion was built up around Jesus, man-made and fallible. True, but the gospel confronts that man-made and fallible system with the same demand and offer as it does the other religions. We do not preach this system built up around Jesus; we preach to it just as we would preach to any other human need. Our message is not the system, but the Saviour.

He is the gospel. The gospel lies in his Person. He himself is the good news. He didn't come to bring the good news. He is the good news. We therefore bring him to East and West and say: The issue is simple. Christ and his kingdom is the issue. Take him direct. You don't have to take our interpretation of Christ, except as you find it helpful in forming your own. Go straight to the Gospels to discover Jesus anew; and if you show us a better interpretation, we shall sit at your feet. The system which we have built up around Christ in the West may be useful and helpful as embodying a collective experience, but it is no integral part of the gospel. Create out of your own experience the corporate expression of that experience. Christ is universal, but he uses local forms to express that universality. We expect you in India, out of your rich cultural and religious past, to bring to the interpretation of the universal Christ something which will greatly enrich the total expression. Especially now that Mahatma Gandhi has lived and died, we think you can interpret Christ in terms in which we are lacking in the West. It will take the sons of men to interpret the Son of Man.

I know that there is still left in the minds of some of my readers a feeling that there is a presumption at the very basis of this presentation—the presumption that "there are many religions; there is but one gospel." That is a presumption. But there we stand; God helping us we can do no other. We have seen and still see in Jesus the gospel —the good news that men everywhere need, and especially ourselves. For this is an evangelism that evangelizes the evangelists. It sends us to our knees even when we proclaim it with most certainty to others. So that at the heart of the proclamation there is a deep humility. The certainty is not founded on the certainty of attainment, but upon the certainty of obtainment. That certainty is rooted in grateful humility, not spiritual pride. This the Mahatma never understood, hence the long controversy.

But there was another factor at the basis of the controversy with the Christians. It was over the mass conversion of the depressed classes. While the Mahatma was opposed to mass conversions, he now and then let drop little things that led us to believe that he thought conversion might be allowable in certain specified cases. He talked as though he were totally opposed, and yet there were exceptions in his mind, I believe. How could he hold otherwise, for he himself was a mighty converter—"the greatest converter of us all," I laughingly told him one day—for he was trying to convert the British empire to his views. He says so specifically:

Conversion of a nation that has consciously or unconsciously preyed upon another far more numerous, far more ancient, and no less cultured than itself is worth any amount of risk. I have deliberately used the word conversion, for my ambition is no less than to convert the British people through nonviolence and thus make them see the wrong they have done to India.[1]

Obviously, the Mahatma was literally the greatest converter of us all and converted the British to a willing consent to India's independence—no mean accomplishment. But Mahatma Gandhi was totally and unequivocally opposed to the conversion of the depressed classes to any faith other than the one they were brought up in.

This position is understandable. Mahatma Gandhi saw the possibility, and the actuality, of mass conversions being used for political ends through communal representation. When this controversy was going on, communal representation, reservation of seats in legislatures, was assigned according to the numbers of the different religious communities—Hindus, Moslems, Sikhs, Christians. Numbers counted, and political power could be gained through mass conversions. The balance of power in the country could be swung through mass conversions of the seventy million untouchables. These mass conversions to Islam or Christianity would come from the Hindu fold. Their balance of power in the country was threatened by it. No wonder the Hindus were alarmed and up in arms. Mahatma Gandhi became the spokesman of that protest and that endeavor to save the untouchables from leaving the Hindu fold. His remedy was to wipe out untouchability and amalgamate the untouchables among the regularly accepted Hindus. He led a mighty movement that swept the country and was responsible for many endeavors for their uplift. Everybody wanted the outcastes. Dr. Ambedkar, leader of the depressed classes, told me, "The Moslems have not only offered us earth, but heaven as well, if we come over to them." The Sikhs built a college in Bombay to receive outcastes, a big bid for them. It was an unseemly scramble for power under the guise of religious conversion.

The Christian Church and the missionaries came under the same suspicion of a mass conversion movement for communal ends. Much

[1] Letter to Lord Irwin, March, 1930.

of this was unfounded. Both Indian Christians and missionaries put out statements saying that they had no desire to use a movement of conversion for communal ends. It was purely religious. But during the struggle of independence it was not at all clear where the Christians stood. Some Indian Christians joined the Non-co-operation Movement; many stood aloof. Some missionaries openly declared their sympathy; the larger part leaned toward the retention of the British occupancy, afraid of what would happen to the Christian movement if independence came. The national leaders knew this; and some of them openly expressed themselves, saying that Christian missions, as now carried on, would not be allowed under swaraj, or independence. Gandhiji put it: "Christian missionaries come to India under the shadow—or if you like, under the protection—of a temporal power, and it creates an impassible bar." They seemed, in the minds of many nationalists, to be allied to imperialism. This, in many cases, was not true, for many thought the pledge of neutrality in coming to India meant they would have to be silent. The silence was taken for consent to things as they were. Under the shadow of mis-understanding the controversy over conversion was carried on for many years. An entire book of three hundred pages, entitled *Christian Missions, Their Place in India,* by M. K. Gandhi, is excerpts from *Young India* and the *Harijan,* his papers. In these articles Mahatmaji says that one should "not even inwardly pray for the conversion of another." In reply to a Polish professor as to how materialism may be fought, he said: "Well, it is no use trying to fight these forces without giving up the idea of conversion, which I assure you is the deadliest poison that ever sapped the fountain of truth." He also complained that medical work among the sick and suffering was offered as a bait for conversions, and education was offered with the same purpose in view.

During this period of controversy I went with two friends, Rev. S. Aldis and Principal David Moses of Hislop College, Nagpur, to interview the Mahatma at Wardha regarding conversion. I said something like this:

"Suppose a man should be inwardly convinced that Christ is the one to whom he should give his allegiance. He needn't change his dress, or his name; he could stand in the stream of India's culture and life and interpret Christ in a framework of India's heritage. If you will allow such a man to stay in his home without disability as an open, baptized member of the Christian Church, then as far as some of us are concerned—and I think I represent the leading Indian Christians in this—we are willing to see the Christian community as a separate political entity fade out, leaving a moral and spiritual and social entity, the Christian Church, to contribute its power to India's uplift and redemption."

The Mahatma thoughtfully replied: "If my son should become a Christian under the conditions you have mentioned, then I would keep him as a member of my home without penalty or disability."

"That is personal," I replied. "Would you recommend it to India?"

He replied: "I would. And if you take the position you now take, then most of the objections to Christianity would fade out of the mind of India."

As we went away in the car, the three of us went over the whole interview together to see if we had it straight, for we saw it was very important. For the first time he had come out with a clear-cut approval of conversion under certain conditions. We agreed that the above was what had passed between us. The interview was published, and six months later a secretary of the Mahatma published in a daily paper that the interview had been misunderstood and misrepresented. The three of us signed a statement in reply saying: "If Stanley Jones misunderstood, then we all three misunderstood and equally, for we are all agreed that this is exactly what was said on both sides." What had happened? Obviously the statement of the Mahatma to us was very important, and leading Hindus must have recognized it as such. Conversion was allowable, according to the Mahatma. They must have brought pressure on the secretary, so that, with or without the Mahatma's knowledge and consent, a retraction was issued—Gandhiji did not approve of conversion.

But I am persuaded that this did represent the Mahatma's mind, for it was sincerely and straightforwardly said without hesitation. And the conditions I laid down for the conversion cleared the objections in the Mahatma's mind. He disliked converts losing the Indian culture and becoming denationalized, and he feared the loss of political power to Hindus through conversions. Here I was saying that the Indian Christian convert need not be denationalized, and that the Christian community as a separate political entity might fade out. In that case there need be no fear of political use of conversions to gain political power. These were his basic objections to conversions; and when they were met, he unhesitatingly approved of conversion.

This whole controversy has been very painful and very purifying.

It has made us as missionaries search our hearts and our methods and motives. And if we are honest, we find ourselves not without blame. Our converts were too often denationalized, identifying Christianity with Westernism; we did lay too much stress on quantity rather than quality in accepting mass conversions; and it was often done without adequate preparation; and we have used medical aid and education as a bait for conversion—not often, but too often to be guiltless. The Mahatma's criticisms across the years, some of them as biting as acid, should make us better and our movement a more Christian movement. They were uttered in love, and we should take them in love. For a strange thing happened: Through all these years of controversy and acid criticism there has been an absence of estrangement between the Mahatma and the missionaries. They clung to each other when they couldn't understand each other. It is true that one missionary called the Mahatma "Enemy No. 1 of the Depressed Classes," and another missionary tried to get the authorities of Canada to keep me out of Canada because I was "a friend of Gandhi," but this was rare. On the whole they knew they belonged together, for they had so much in common, and there was an affinity between them. The way the missionaries and the Indian Christians would keep coming back to the Mahatma and would ask the same questions over and over showed that there was something that hadn't come out; the matter wasn't final, and they belonged together. They did.

When I returned to India a year ago, I found the missionaries and some Indian Christians troubled as to their position in independent India. Would the missionaries be allowed in the new India, and would the Indian Christians be allowed to evangelize? At one stage the Mahatma said that the work of conversion would not be allowed in a free India. I wrote in the little paper which I edit, *The Fellowship:*

We note that you say that evangelism will probably not be allowed in a free India. You have taught us a method which, in that case, we would be compelled to use, though reluctantly, namely, the method of nonviolent civil disobedience. Christians have gone to jail before over this issue, and they could gladly do it again.

The only cutting word I ever received from the Mahatma was in answer to this statement. I told him later that I did not show his reply to my colleagues at the Ashram, "for I didn't want them to see this Mahatma Gandhi but the real one." At which we both laughed, and the incident was dismissed and almost forgotten.

There was general uncertainty over the relationships of the Christian movement and the national movement. So I went to the national leaders for clarification. I told them I was going to speak to large missionary gatherings in the South and in the North at the hill stations, and I wanted a clarification to take to them. Would the missionaries be allowed to function in the new India? If so, would they be tolerated or welcomed as partners in the remaking of India?

The reply of Vallabhai Patel, the Home Member of the government, in charge of the police and having the say as to who should or should not come into India, was very important, so I waited with breathless interest. The future of a whole movement in India rested in a way upon it. He replied:

Let the missionaries go on as they have been going on—serving the suffering through their hospitals and dispensaries, the poor through their schools. Let them serve the people in a selfless way. They can even carry on their propaganda in a peaceful manner. But don't let them use a religious movement to build up communal power through mass conversions.

I explained to him that, in common with most of the Indian Christian leaders, I was opposed to communal representation, and we would be the first to repudiate it if the country was organized on some basis other than communal representation, so we had no desire to build up communal power through conversion. It was degrading to the country, and it was degrading to religion. "Then," he said, "let the missionaries throw in their lot with India and make India their home." This was so straightforward, so sincere, and so reassuring that, as one missionary doctor put it, "it lifted a great load off my heart."

I then went to C. Rajagopalachari, then minister of industry and now governor general of India. His reply was:

You have a legal right to convert; but since conversion is such a divisive thing in India, I would suggest as a matter of strategy that you dim it and serve the people until conditions turn to normal. In that case you will not only be welcome; you will be welcomed with gratitude.

The next important man visited was Abul Kalam Azad, the Moslem minister for education, an important man, since we have so many educational institutions in India. His reply was warm and friendly:

Don't use the word "tolerate." There is no question of tolerating the missionaries. We have no point at issue with the missionaries except the one question of mass conversions being used for political ends. When there is a moral and spiritual change, then there is no question of the right to outer change; but where there is no moral and spiritual change involved, then it raises questions as to motives.

When I gave my views on this, he said:

We know what the missionaries have done for India and the rest of the world, especially for the Near East through your colleges, so we welcome you to the new India.

Then the most important man in the government, the prime minister, Jawaharlal Nehru:

I don't quite know what is involved in being "welcomed as partners" in the making of the new India, but we will welcome anyone who throws himself in with India and makes India his home.

These statements could not have been finer and more reassuring. So I took them to the missionary conventions at Kodaikanal and Landour, both of them hill stations with about five hundred persons in each convention. They unanimously put out declarations of their attitudes, one of which was as follows:

This group of missionaries, numbering about five hundred, representing many denominations and nationalities, assembled in the Landour, Mussoorie, Convention, wishes to express its gratitude that India's independence is at hand.

We are grateful that this independence is coming into being with the consent and co-operation of Britain. We believe that this amicable separation will mean that these two nations will be bound together by closer ties in the future.

We are aware of the difficulties ahead, but we are more aware of the possibilities. We pledge ourselves to help in every legitimate way in the solution of those difficulties and in the realization of those possibilities.

We believe that this new freedom will mean a new freedom to develop the latent possibilities of this land and that an era of progress and prosperity will begin. We further believe that a free India will be a great asset in furthering world freedom and peace. For in spite of the present upset, we know that the genius of India is peace. We believe that this genius will reassert itself and that the collective will of this nation will eventually bring peace and unity into being.

We would be servants of Christ and of India and would identify ourselves with the people of this land—their sorrows our sorrows, their joys our joys, and their successes our successes.

We regret that the political life of the country is organized on a communal basis. If the Christian community has been compelled to accept communal representation, it does so with no inner belief in its validity, and, we are convinced, it will be the first to repudiate it if another and better basis is found.

We believe in the inherent right of individuals and groups to outer conversion where there is an inner conversion, but we have no desire now, nor have we had any desire in the past, to build up communal power for political ends through religious conversion. We think it debasing to religion and to politics to use a moral and spiritual movement for political ends.

We pledge ourselves to support in every legitimate way the lawfully established government set up to serve the interests of the people. We will give it the best we have. We hope that the government will feel free to call on us to help make India the land of our common hopes and prayers.

These declarations were sent to the leading Congressmen and to the newspapers and drew a great deal of attention—and apparent gratitude. What had happened? These two movements—the Nationalist movement and the Christian movement, especially the missionary phase of it—were drawing together. The period of estrangement was over. They would now work together for the making of a new India. That was one of the most important events that have happened in the missionary world in this century. It meant a new identification with India and her needs.

I think the Christian movement could subscribe to something like this: (1) We have no ulterior motives in our work. When we do medical or educational work, we do it because we believe in it as such. If no one were ever converted through healing the sick and educating youth, we would still do both, as things that stand in their own right and not a means to something else. Jesus didn't heal people on condition that they follow him. He healed them because they needed to be healed. If along with it they chose to follow him, he would welcome them. If along with the coming of healing and education there are those who feel disposed to follow Christ, we will welcome them, but we do not use these services as baits. That would be degrading to the service and to us and to the people who took it. (2) We pledge ourselves and the country that we will take individuals and groups into the Christian Church only when they manifest an inner moral and spiritual change that justifies the outer change. On the whole this has been our policy and practice, and we reaffirm it with renewed dedication.

We are grateful that the main bone of contention, namely, building up communal power through mass conversions, has been removed through the removal of communal representation itself. Hereafter men and women will not be chosen for public office on a communal basis by a communal electorate according to communal numbers. That is the position the Christian leaders have taken all along; at least they expressed their willingness to accept it. In doing so they showed a high patriotism, and this was recognized by the country at the time. Now that this is done, the tensions about conversions should let down.

The fact is that in the Draft Constitution for an independent India there is this sentence: "Subject to public order, morality, and health . . . all persons are equally entitled to freedom of conscience and the right freely to profess, practice, and propagate religion." Nothing could be clearer. The right to convert is conceded, for there is no point in being able to propagate one's faith if there can be no acceptance of it by conversion to it. There is one fly in this ointment, for the Central Provinces government has made an act that no one can change his faith unless he appears before a magistrate and declares his intention. After police investigation the magistrate decides whether he can change his faith. This obviously cuts across the constitution; for while it does not forbid conversion, it makes it so difficult as to be well-nigh impossible. Over against this can be placed the fact that the enactment has been interpreted by Dr. Rajendra Parshad, president of the Constituent Assembly, as not applying to ordinary conversions, but only to forced conversions; that it was promulgated to cover forced conversions to Islam; and that the law was only temporary. On the whole this issue of conversion has been clarified, and a new day of understanding has begun. I was introduced recently to a non-Christian audience by a chairman who said:

Two things have hitherto hindered us from listening with any degree of openness to a man like Stanley Jones. (1) We were afraid that mass conversions would be used for communal ends. (2) We didn't know whether the missionaries were the agents of imperialism or not. Both of these issues have been clarified. Communal representation has been wiped out, so conversions cannot now be used for communal ends. And we now see that the missionaries are with this new independent India. So we listen gladly to what Stanley Jones has to say.

I felt in this last year that the period of tension with the Mahatma had passed; that the issues were clarified; that while we did not agree in many things, we were working for the same purpose, the making of a new India.

Many things remain unresolved. On the part of some of us we are still puzzled why a man of such moral and spiritual sincerity as Mahatma Gandhi could fasten on Rama, a deified prince of the past, and make him the center of his worship, for the Mahatma surpassed Rama in every possible way—intellectually, morally, spiritually. It is true that he said he used the word "Rama" for "God." Perhaps it becomes more easy to understand when we remember that in childhood he had a fear of ghosts and spirits, and Rambha, a nursemaid, suggested as a remedy for this fear the repetition of Ramanama, the name of Rama. So he says: "At a tender age I began repeating Ramanama to cure my fear of ghosts and spirits. This of course was short-lived, but the good seed sown in childhood was not sown in vain. I think it is due to the seed sown by that good woman, Rambha, that today Ramanama is an infallible remedy for me." This seed sown in childhood became a part of his subconscious life. He never dissected the idea; he distilled out of it a victory. It became "an infallible remedy" for him over the real fears of later life. He transcended the means. His spirit was so great that he could take a mistaken idea and make it contribute. There was no unreality or hypocrisy; he saw it worked, and for him it did. But it was his spirit that made it work, and not the thing itself. There was no potency in Ramanama, but there was potency in the man who uttered it. "He was more right when he was wrong than we are when we are right." Mahatma Gandhi was more right in uttering the wrong idea of Ramanama because of his spirit than we often are in uttering the name of Christ because of our spirit. He distilled nectar out of inadequate ideas because of the spirit that did the distilling.

Take another puzzling fact: The Mahatma, believing in and practicing nonviolence, made the center of his affection and loyalty a book based on a philosophical justification of the use of force, namely, the Bhagavad-Gita. The Mahatma interprets the battle between the Pandavas and the Kauravas as a spiritual battle and not a battle between two clans as stated. He says: "The fight is there, but the fight as it is going on within. The Pandavas and Kauravas are the forces of good and evil within. The war is the war between Jekyll and Hyde, God and Satan, going on in the human breast." The difficulty with that explanation is that there is no moral distinction that can be made between the Pandavas and the Kauravas. They were morally indistinguishable—six in one and half a dozen in the other. Dr. Kagawa says: "But Arjuna's views [in hesitating to fight] seem to be superior to Krishna's [in urging him to fight]." The Mahatma replies: "Then according to you the disciple was greater than the master." And he leaves it at that. "Spiritualization is the first refuge of the skeptical mind." But the Mahatma's mind was not a skeptical mind. It believed mightily in nonviolence—believed in it so much that he could get nonviolence out of a book based on the philosophical defense of violence. Again he was right when he was wrong. He not only made violent people nonviolent; he made violent discourses nonviolent—and did it by his amazing spirit. And here I am not merely playing with words. This is a sober fact: we find an amazing spirit transforming everything he touched into his own likeness. The Gita became Gandhian. "There is no violence here," pointing to his breast; "how can there be violence there?" pointing to the book. So you do not argue; you admire and love the soul that can find nonviolence even in the Gita, even as we have loved and admired Christians who see more in the Old Testament characters than the account would warrant. They read back into the account their own Christian ideas and attitudes. So the Mahatma has read back into the Gita his own nonviolence.

As Mahatma Gandhi was recuperating after an operation for appendicitis performed by a British surgeon in a Poona hospital, having been temporarily released from jail for the operation, I asked if I could see him at 6 A.M. in order to get back to Bombay for my engagements. He was gracious enough to wire: "Yes, please do come." As I paced the station platform before daybreak thinking of what I should say to him, as he would be taking up the threads of his work again upon his release, I saw the parallel between him and the apostles as they said, "Lord, wilt thou at this time restore again the kingdom to Israel?" They wanted the restoration of the kingdom to Israel, just as the Mahatma was desiring the restoration of the kingdom to India. But Jesus offered the apostles a bigger kingdom than they had dreamed—a world kingdom—if they would be his witness: "It is not for you to know times or seasons, which the Father hath set within his own authority. But ye shall receive power, when the Holy Spirit is come upon you: and ye shall be my witnesses both in Jerusalem, and in all Judaea, and Samaria, and unto the uttermost parts of the earth" (Acts 1:7-8 American Standard Version). They asked for a restoration of a national kingdom, and Jesus offered them a world kingdom if they would witness to him. I saw the parallels. So I said to the Mahatma:

"I am going to the West tomorrow. Could you give me a message to the Western world as to how we should live this Christian life?"

He thought a moment and said: "Such a message cannot be given by word of mouth; it can only be lived. All I can do is to live it—that will be my message."

I was deeply moved by this realistic attitude and saw how very right he was. Then I added: "If you have no message for me, I think I got one for you as I walked the railway station platform this morning." I called attention to the parallels. "The apostles and you want a restoration of a kingdom—and rightly. The restoration of the kingdom will come to India. It is bound to come, and I want to see it come. But there is a greater kingdom awaiting you. We of the West are sick of the methods of militarism. We need a leader—one who could lead us on a new road away from militarism and war. You are an apostle of nonviolence. You could be that leader. We need you. In order to be that leader it would be necessary, I think, to appeal to us through the faith we hold. We will need a spiritual center for the movement. Jesus, I believe, can be that center—inherently so, and through the fact that we of the West hold to him at least a nominal allegiance. If you will give a clear-cut witness to Jesus, then a world kingdom is awaiting you. By a clear-cut witness to Jesus I do not mean coming out and being a baptized Christian. I leave that to your guidance. I mean a clear-cut emphasis upon Jesus as the center of your nonviolent movement among us of the West. This world kingdom awaits you. Will you take it?"

I really meant it, for it was the period between the first and second world wars, and we were drifting toward war. I felt that the Mahatma could lead us and was really our hope to avert war. He never really answered the question. But he sat there with tears in his eyes. Those tears seemed to say: "I wish I could do it. But the time isn't ripe for me to try it. I must demonstrate the power of nonviolence here in India. Then maybe the world will take it." He quietly said: "I can only demonstrate it here." And that was all. All? Here again he was profoundly right. For if he had gone to Europe, as I hoped he would, and tried to lead us out of war, it would have been premature. He hadn't demonstrated the effectiveness of Satyagraha; independence had not been won. And Europe hadn't reached the bottom of despair with militarism. She still thought there was power in military might to decide things. Complete disillusionment had not come. It is now about to come. For Europe and the West are seized with despair and fear as to what will happen if militarism takes the saddle again and atomic bombs are used. It will be the ride to collective death.

Mahatma Gandhi and I bowed in prayer and commended the whole proposal to God. And God may yet answer the request I made for the Mahatma to lead us out of war through a witness to Jesus as the center of that movement away from war. Now that the Mahatma has died a martyr to his cause and the ideas wrapped up in his frail body have been loosed and have become the possession of humanity, it may be that his entering into a world kingdom is at hand. That possibility we shall study in the next chapter.

At any rate the other half of the proposition has come true in very large measure. I asked him to give his witness to Christ, and he never promised that he would. But he has! In ways some of us never dreamed he would. He spent years criticizing the system of missions and the methods of the Christians, but in the end he furthered the cause of Christ. The man who was most critical turned out to be most constructive—constructive at the place where it counted most: at the place of Christ. The system can change, but the Saviour cannot. He must stand unchanged. He has. And a flood of fresh light has been thrown on him in the death of the Mahatma. A flood of statements from non-Christians poured forth from the soul of India likening the Mahatma to Christ in life and death. We don't always agree with those statements, and yet they reveal the soul of a nation and the soul of Gandhi. The editor of The Hindu in an editorial the day after his death refers to Mahatma Gandhi as "the second Saviour." A newspaper item from Nagpur after his death said: "How Christlike was his end, was the universal comment." M. Syed Hussain, India's ambassador-delegate to Egypt, said: "The savior of India has been crucified. He is gone; it means that India will walk eternally in the shadow of his cross." The Burmese ambassador to India, U Win, said: "The world has suffered an irreparable loss today. Just as Jesus Christ suffered to save erring humanity, so has Mahatmaji suffered now." Mr. Gopinath Bardoloi, prime minister, Assam: "Posterity will recognize Mahatmaji as one of the greatest teachers of humanity in the same way as people look on Jesus Christ." Sir A. Ramaswami Mudaliar, prime minister of Mysore: "Mahatmaji has indeed been a new messiah to this world." Maulana Mohammed Tayebulla, president of Assam Congress Committee: "Mahatmaji, the apostle of nonviolence, has fallen like Christ, a martyr to the sacred cause of truth and peace." Sir Muthiah Chettiar in the Madras Assembly: "He has been aptly described as Christ returned to earth." Dr. M. R. Jayakar, former judge, Federal Court of India: "This foul assassination of the Mahatma marks the climax of similarity which he valued so dearly between his mission and that of Jesus Christ. They are brothers in martyrdom." T. Krishnaswami Aiyer, retired chief justice, Travancore state: "From out of the sacrifice of the great leader emerged the independence of India. Christ was nailed to the cross. The whole world was permeated with the ideals of one of which Christ was the symbol. Even so, Mahatma Gandhi will outlive his death as the symbol of peace and tolerance."

And so one of the most Christlike men in history was not called a Christian at all. And the man who fought Christian civilization, so-called, furthered the real thing. God uses many instruments, and he has used Mahatma Gandhi to help Christianize unchristian Christianity.

CHAPTER VI

"My Experiments with Truth"

MAHATMA GANDHI wrote the story of his life; but instead of calling it an autobiography, he called it *My Experiments with Truth.* For many years I never caught the significance of that title. It is really the key to his whole life. It is the clue to his power.

A governor of one of the provinces said to me, "Gandhi was a gambler; he gambled his life on truth." He was an astonishing gambler. He would throw his very life upon the table in any issue he felt called upon to face. He was a reckless gambler. And yet he was a man who gambled only when he was sure of winning! Before he gambled, he had experimented to see what would work and what would not work. So he followed the wave of probability, which became to him the wave of certainty. Here was a man who apparently rejected the whole of the accomplishments of Western science, and yet who adopted the very center of that science, namely, experimentation. He applied experimentation to moral and spiritual laws, while Western science occupies itself largely with experimentation with physical laws.

Gandhi was an experimenter in many realms, but he was primarily an experimenter of the spirit and its laws. But he demanded experimentation even regarding sacred texts. When he was experimenting with foods, he said:

Two or three have sent me the identical text [from the Ayur-Vedic writings] against taking honey mixed with hot water and pronouncing dire results. When I have asked them whether they had verified the text from their own experience, they were silent. My own experience of taking honey mixed with hot water extends to more than four years. I have experienced no ill effects whatever.[1]

Here was an important statement and attitude: everything, including sacred scriptures, must be subject to experimentation and verification.

[1] *Young India,* Aug. 15, 1929.

To take anything on blind faith was wrong. This is revolutionary. It is like the seed of a peepul tree, which, when dropped into the cracks of a temple, will leave it in ruins around the foot of the growing tree. This idea of Gandhi, if applied, will leave mere dogmatisms not based on reality a ruin around the base of growing truth.

Gandhi was a gambler, but a cautious gambler. Like the elephant, which, when about to pass over a questionable bridge, tries it with his forefeet before venturing his full weight, so Gandhi cautiously tried out certain principles; and, when convinced they were truth, he would fling himself upon them with abandon. And he would not recommend them to others until he had tried them: "It has been a rule of my life never to ask anyone to do anything which I had not tried out in practice myself."

He tells of reading Ruskin's *Unto This Last* and how he summed up its teachings.

This is how I understand Ruskin's teaching: (1) The good of the individual is contained in the good of all. (2) A lawyer's labor has the same value as the barber's, inasmuch as all have the same right to earn their livelihood from their labor. (3) A life of labor, i.e., of the tiller of the soil and handicraftsman, is the life worth living. The first I knew. The second I had dimly realized. The third had never occurred to me. Ruskin made it as clear as possible for me that the second and the third were contained in the first. I awoke with the dawn, ready to reduce these principles to practice.

Then followed a lifelong devotion to simplicity of life and hand labor. But note that last sentence: "I awoke with the dawn, ready to reduce these principles to practice." Many of us would have talked and debated and consulted interminably. Gandhi decided at dawn to reduce the principles to practice. That is the essential difference in Gandhi; he acted on what he saw to be truth. He didn't see all truth, but he acted on what he saw, and that made the difference.

Take the Cross. Mahatma Gandhi did not see in the Cross what the convinced Christian sees, namely, that God was in Christ reconciling the world unto himself and that he was bearing our sins in his body on a tree. Gandhi did not see that. But he did see that you can take on yourself suffering, and not give it, and thus conquer the heart of another. That he did see in the Cross, and that he put into practice, and put it into practice on a national scale. The difference then is this: we as Christians saw more in the Cross than Gandhi and put it into operation less; Gandhi saw less in the Cross than we and put it into practice more. We left the Cross a doctrine; Gandhi left it a deed. Therefore Gandhi, with his half-light and fuller practice, goes in power beyond us who have fuller light and half-practice. God therefore accepts his operative deed and entrusts him with power, while God can use in only a limited way our faith which is minus the operative deed. God apparently has to pass by the orthodoxy and use the orthopraxy. Do not misunderstand me. I do not minimize right belief; it is necessary. But "not every one that saith unto me, Lord, Lord, shall enter into the kingdom of heaven; but he that doeth the will of my Father which is in heaven."

A nominally Christian world expounds truth, and Gandhi experiments with it. That makes the difference.

Take another fact. Mahatma Gandhi did not see the person of Christ as the real Christian does. He was dim at that place. But certain principles of the Sermon on the Mount did grip him, and he forthwith put them into practice—overcoming evil with good, hate by love. In the practice of those principles he discovered and lived by the person of Christ, however dimly and unconsciously. "Lord, when saw we thee an hungred and fed thee? . . . Inasmuch as ye have done it unto one of the least of these my brethren, ye have done it unto me." Gandhi was one of those who in doing it to "the least of these" was doing it unto Christ, however unconsciously. He discovered a dim Christ through the deed, and we discover a dim Christ through the doctrine. We can only discover the real Christ through the doctrine and the deed.

The Gandhi who experimented with what he saw to be truth became the Gandhi of experience. He experienced what he acted on. He did not see everything, but what he did see became vital through a willingness to experiment with it. He refused to preach anything he had not tried. When I urged him to go to Europe before the war, hoping that his very presence there would be a call to peace instead of war, his reply was simple: "I have not demonstrated peace in my country; how can I preach it to Europe?" Somebody has said that "all great literature is autobiography." Then all great preaching is the sharing of an operative fact. Gandhi's words had weight, for they had the content of experimentation in them. When people came to him with educational theories, he would say: "Here is the money. Go and experiment and see how your ideas work; and if they work well, we will adopt them." Thus he came to the ideas underlying basic education which were worked out under his inspiration. The basis of basic education is that you practice what you learn. It is education for life, and life here in India. In basic education the pupils are to be self-sustaining in food, clothing, cooking, sanitation, and community service. While they study, they are to be self-sustaining.

One of his important statements is this:

The world rests upon the bedrock of Satya or Truth. Asatya meaning Untruth, also means "non-existent"; and Satya, or Truth, means "that which is." If untruth does not so much as exist, its victory is out of the question. And Truth being "that which is" can never be destroyed. This is the doctrine of Satyagraha in a nutshell.[2]

If truth is that which is, then the business of life is to identify yourself with it; then the sum total of reality will be behind you. But you do not identify yourself with truth when you accept it only as idea; you identify yourself with it as a life identification, a putting of truth into your life attitudes and your life acts. Then you are invincible. But if you are identified with any untruth, then you are vulnerable and weak. The universe won't sustain you. Gandhi had only a very few basic life principles, but he made them walk—and what a walk!

[2] C. F. Andrews, ed., *Mahatma Gandhi—His Own Story*, p. 225.

CHAPTER VII

The Center of Gandhi's Contribution--Satyagraha

THE word "Satyagraha" seems as foreign to us as the idea underlying it. It literally means "truth force," or "truth power." This idea and practice was at the center of Gandhi's life and is the center of his contribution to the world. All else is marginal compared to this. The quintessence of Gandhism is Satyagraha. If we don't get this, we have missed the meaning of his life and death.

I would sum up the five great contributions which Mahatma Gandhi gave to the world as follows: (1) a new spirit and technique— Satyagraha; (2) the emphasis that the moral universe is one and that the morals of individual, group, and nation must be the same; (3) his insistence that the means and the ends must be consistent; (4) the fact that he held no ideals he did not embody or was not in the process of embodying; (5) a willingness to suffer and die for his principles. These are the five great things he gave, but the greatest of these is Satyagraha.

The idea of Satyagraha slowly evolved and then took possession of him. The germ of the idea was given to him in a Gujarati hymn. He says of it: "Its precepts—return good for evil—became my guiding principle. It became such a passion with me that I began numerous experiments in it." The hymn:

> For a bowl of water give a goodly meal;
> For a kindly greeting bow thou down with zeal;
> For a simple penny pay thou back with gold;
> If thy life be rescued, life do not withhold.
> Thus the words and actions of the wise regard;
> Every little service tenfold they reward.
> But the truly noble know all men as one,
> And return with gladness good for evil done.

The germ of the idea came from this hymn. "But it was the New Testament that fixed it in my heart," says Gandhi.

The Sermon on the Mount went straight to my heart. The verses, "But I say unto you, That ye resist not evil: but whosoever shall smite thee on thy right cheek, turn to him the other also. And if any man . . . take away thy coat, let him have thy cloke also," delighted me beyond measure. . . . That renunciation was the highest form of religion appealed to me greatly.

When a missionary, Dr. S. W. Clemes, asked the Mahatma years ago what book or person had influenced him most, he replied: "The Bible, Ruskin, and Tolstoy." In later years he would have undoubtedly added the Gita. Tolstoy, with his insistence that the Sermon on the Mount be taken literally and acted on, helped to confirm the idea of the Gujarati hymn and to expound it. It was Ruskin's *Unto This Last* that made him decide on a life of simplicity. This is noteworthy: a book out of the war-ridden West—the New Testament— turned him against war, and a book out of the materialistic, complicated civilization of Europe—Ruskin's—turned him toward simplicity. He reduced life to its bare necessities. *Unto This Last* put together religion and service: "As you did it to one of the least of these my brethren, you did it to me" (Revised Standard Version). His religion would be a serving of God through a serving of men. He would be nonviolent; he would be simple; and he would serve God through humanity. Thus was his working faith formed.

But it was an incident that precipitated all these gathering elements into a fixed life attitude.

I recall particularly one experience that changed the course of my life. That experience fell to my lot seven days after I arrived in South Africa. On the train I had a first-class ticket, but not a bed ticket. At Maritzburg, where the beddings were issued, the guard came and turned me out and asked me to go to the van compartment. I would not go, and the train steamed away leaving me in the shivering cold. Now the creative experience comes there. I was afraid for my very life. I entered the dark waiting room. There was a white man in the room. I was afraid of him. What is my duty? I asked myself. Should I go back to India, or should I go forward, with God as my helper, and face whatever was in store for me? I decided to stay and suffer. My active nonviolence began from that date. And God put me through the test during that journey. I was severely assaulted by the coach attendant for my moving from the seat he had given me. That was one of the richest experiences of my life.[1]

[1] *Harijan,* Dec. 10, 1938.

There were two other influences that helped shape Mahatma Gandhi's ideas and attitudes. Thoreau's essay "Civil Disobedience," expounding the fact that a man must obey his own conscience even against the will of his fellow citizens and be ready to undergo imprisonment in consequence, for after all it was only his body, but not his spirit, which was in custody, arrived at a critical moment in South Africa and greatly appealed to him. Concerning this Gandhiji says:

The statement that I derived my idea of civil disobedience from the writings of Thoreau is wrong. The resistance to authority in South Africa was well advanced before I got the essay of Thoreau on civil disobedience. But the movement was then known as passive resistance. As it was incomplete, I had coined the word Satyagraha for the Gujarati readers. When I saw the title of Thoreau's great essay, I began the use of the phrase to explain our struggle to the English readers. But I found that even civil disobedience failed to convey the full meaning of the struggle. I therefore adopted the phrase "civil resistance." Nonviolence was always an integral part of our struggle.

Another influence was his observation in 1909 of the British suffragettes and their methods involving imprisonment for the gaining of their goals.

Here was a confluence of influence which God used to mold a mighty instrument of his purposes for this age: a Gujarati hymn from India, a New Testament from Palestine, a book from Russia, a pamphlet from America, a book and the suffragette influence from Britain, and then two men in South Africa, a coach attendant and a white occupant of a waiting room. All these combine to push Gandhi as by a hand of destiny into the arena of the twentieth century to fight one of the noblest fights that have been fought by man for the liberation of man. They combined to make Gandhi the greatest revolutionary of the age—and the most gentle and humane. Clemenceau, the Tiger, once said: "When the Christian decides to be a Christian, then the real revolution begins." Gandhi, although not a Christian, decided to take a Christian attitude—the overcoming of evil with good—and there the real revolution began. When Gandhiji began to apply a New Testament principle to public affairs, then that was revolutionary. During the struggle for independence I was giving a series of lectures to non-Christians. Two police plainclothes men were down in front taking shorthand notes of what I was saying to see if there was anything seditious. There was, for I was speaking on the Sermon on the Mount! The Sermon on the Mount is revolutionary when in the hands of Gandhi he applies it as a technique and an attitude to public affairs. I was applying it verbally, and therefore it was nonseditious; but Gandhi was applying it vitally, and therefore it was seditious. In the hands of Gandhi the New Testament = T.N.T. In our hands very often it becomes a soporific. The little girl was nearer to the meaning when she said: "Barbara, I tell you the New Testament does not end with Timothy; it ends with Revolutions." But with us it often ends where one described a certain conference as ending: "It was a very resolutionary conference." Gandhi turned our resolutions into revolutions, by the simple method of applying them.

But there was another strain that went into the making of Gandhi and his revolution. It was his conception of truth. Perhaps in the end it may be seen to be the most important element. For a long time the meaning of it seemed to elude me. Now it is clearer. He identified truth and God. He said:

I do not regard God as a Person. Truth for me is God, and God's Law and God are not different things or facts, in the sense that an earthly king and his law are different. Because God is an Idea, Law Himself. He and His Law abide everywhere and govern everything.[2]

Again and again he said: "I do not say God is Truth; I say, Truth is God." Here he seems to rule out a personal God and make him identical with an impersonal Law. And yet that isn't quite accurate, for he called God "Law Himself." If he meant that God was impersonal, why should he say "Law Himself" instead of "Itself"? Besides, he tells about what happened just before going on a twenty-one-day fast:

About 12 o'clock in the night something wakes me up suddenly, and some voice—within or without, I cannot say—whispers, "Thou must go on fast." "How many days?" I ask. The voice again says: "Twenty-one days." "When does it begin?" I ask. It says, "You begin tomorrow." . . . That kind of experience has never happened before or after that date. . . . If ever there was a spiritual fast, it was this. . . . It is not possible to see God face to face unless you crucify the flesh.

[2] *Ibid.*, March 23, 1940.

Obviously an impersonal law doesn't speak to you in this personal manner, and you don't want to see a law "face to face." So this law is more than impersonal law; it partakes of the qualities of the personal. Truth to him seems to be identical with this law and also identical with God. To identify himself with truth was to be identified with God, and it would have the surety of a law. The Mahatma believed that if you always did the true thing, you would have the backing of the moral universe. He believed that the stars in their course would work for you. And they would likewise work against all evil. He further held that we and the universe are made for truth: "Truth is the law of our being." If truth is the law of our being, then to act according to it is to fulfill ourselves, and to act or think according to untruth is to disrupt ourselves. The thing to do then is to identify ourselves with truth, do the true thing always, and a true result will follow. Don't bother about results. They take care of themselves. The moral universe guarantees them. All we have to do is to see that we are on the right side of things, and the moral universe takes care of the rest. It reminds one of the statement made to Lincoln during the Civil War, "I hope God is on our side." The reply was: "My concern is whether we are on God's side." Gandhi had one problem in life: In this matter am I on the side of truth? When he decided to adopt two things, truth and nonviolence—one the fact and the other the method of applying the fact—he went forth believing that he had cosmic backing for what he was doing. It gave him an inner steadiness of purpose and a terrific drive— quiet but terrific. For Gandhi felt himself the agent of cosmic forces working through him. "I will not sacrifice Truth and ahimsa [nonviolence] even for the deliverance of my country and my religion," he said.

This is worth noting, for the means of achieving his ends became the all-important thing to him. He could not use a wrong means to get to a right end, for he knew that the means pre-exist in and determine the ends. Hence he was prepared to call off a movement even when it was apparently successful, for he knew that success would turn to ashes if the means did not coincide with truth and nonviolence. Y. G. Krishnamurti says:

He has accepted the law of nonviolence as rigid and as certain as the law that governs the fall of Newton's apple. The uniqueness of the Mahatma is that he has created and kept alive the faith of the people in nonviolence and truth. If President Hoover promises two cars in every garage, Gandhi promises two virtues in every heart.[3]

Gandhi's strategy is truth, and his method is nonviolence.

By restoring truth and love to the status of ultimate realities Gandhi has brought about a revolution in contemporary thought. . . . The saint Gandhi has not wavered in his passionate belief that truth and love are invincible.[4]

When I asked Jawaharlal Nehru what he considered the greatest contribution of Mahatma Gandhi, he replied: "Means and ends must be consistent." Acharya Kripalani named two: "That means must be consistent with the ends in view and that the same moral laws which hold good for the individual hold good for the group and the nation."

In this the Mahatma cuts across a great deal that goes under the form of Christian civilization, and he goes point-blank against the methods of war and the methods of communism. Both of the latter say that the end justifies the means. War and communism both will use any means that gets them to their respective goals. That is right which gets you to your goal, and that is wrong which hinders or obstructs your getting to your goal. Deceit, treachery, trickery, lies, butchery, will be used if they can be used for the supposed right ends. Gandhi knew better. He knew that if you, as a surgeon, used infected instruments, you would leave the patient worse than ever. Every wrong means will return to haunt the user. Like the sorcerer's apprentice who came to his master and said, "Sir, I have called up a spirit, and now I cannot rid myself of it," so every wrong means called in to get to right ends will stay to plague the user.

Take an illustration from the contemporary scene in India. The tribesmen of the frontier have been a thorn in India's side. They live by plunder. The British kept them quiet by force and subsidy, in other words, bribery. The plan of the Congress was to convert these tribesmen through Abdul Ghaffar Khan, "The Frontier Gandhi," and his *Khudai Khidmatgars*, Servants of God. They were well on their way to harnessing their destruction to construction, for these *Khudai Khidmatgars*, or Red Shirts, were amazingly disciplined and constructive. Then came the partition, and the Northwest Frontier

[3] *Gandhi Era*, p. 42.
[4] *Ibid.*, pp. 79-80.

came into Pakistan and with it the problem of the tribesmen living just beyond the frontier. Pakistan has obviously invited, or at least encouraged, them to go into Kashmir to keep Kashmir from going into the Indian union. They have to go through Pakistan to get into Kashmir. Once in Pakistan they are going to be difficult to get out. I'm told that the tribesmen, well-armed and rough, saunter up to a Moslem shop in a Pakistan city, pick out what they want, and walk away without paying, saying as they leave: "*Ham ap ka mahman hain*" —We are your guests. My prediction is that Pakistan is going to rue the day they were invited in to stir up trouble in Kashmir; for once in, they are going to stay in—as unwelcome guests. Use the wrong means, and sooner or later they will plague you.

The greatness of Gandhi consisted in the fact that he would not look at the end results; he would use the right means, and the right result would follow. The universe guaranteed it. He could subscribe wholeheartedly to these familiar lines:

Truth forever on the scaffold, Wrong forever on the throne,
Yet that scaffold sways the Future, and, behind the dim unknown,
Standeth God within the shadow, keeping watch upon his own.

Panoplied with these convictions, Gandhi steps into the arena of India to apply his principles on the widest scale and for the biggest stakes ever attempted by any man. He would win freedom for India by truth and nonviolence. It is true that the historic situation helped in the adoption of nonviolence, for India was a disarmed nation. Arms were licensed only to those who were known supporters of the government. So nonviolence was accepted out of necessity. And yet out of choice. And further: undoubtedly an overruling Providence was using India as a proving ground for a new type of power—the power of soul. But the Mahatma repudiated with all his might the idea that the method of truth and nonviolence was used because you are weak and cowardly. He insisted that it was the method of the strong, and only the method of the strong. He further insisted that it was better to fight than to take up nonviolence through fear or cowardice.

The weapons Gandhi chose were simple: We will match our capacity to suffer against your capacity to inflict the suffering, our soul force against your physical force. We will not hate you, but we will not obey you. Do what you like, and we will wear you down by our capacity to suffer. And in the winning of the freedom we will so appeal to your heart and conscience that we will win you. So ours will be a double victory; we will win our freedom and our captors in the process.

I said the method of the Mahatma was simple, and more, it must be kept simple. You cannot complicate it by mixing in other methods to help it out. For instance, a leading communist of Ceylon said to me: "We communists are prepared to use any method that gets us to our goal—the ballot, passive resistance, or force." Here he revealed a muddled moral mentality. If you submit the issues to the ballot box, you have to abide by the decision of that ballot box. You cannot abandon it if it goes against you and appeal to force. That is not democracy. Nor can you begin using nonviolent passive resistance and, if you find it isn't working, then appeal to force. These methods cancel out each other. You cannot alternately use the moral appeal and, if it doesn't work, then use force; for the one against whom you appeal must know that you are depending on the moral alone and will not abandon it halfway. It must be kept pure. And the Mahatma wisely kept it pure. South Africa taught him to keep his eye single; then his whole body would be full of light. But if his eye became evil (complicated), then the whole body would be full of darkness.

Gandhiji sums up the issues in a statement given to the press on December 4, 1932, after his famous fast unto death:

Those who have to bring about radical changes in human conditions and surroundings cannot do it except by raising a ferment in society. There are only two methods of doing this, violent and nonviolent. Violent pressure is felt on the physical being, and it degrades him who uses it as it depresses the victim, but nonviolent pressure exerted through self-suffering, as by fasting, works in an entirely different way. It touches not the physical body, but it touches and strengthens the moral fiber of those against whom it is directed.

When the Mahatma stepped on the scene, the movement for independence was underground. It manifested itself in bombs and assassinations and a sullen hate. In those early days I sat with a man who came to talk to me about spiritual things. As he was about to go, he remarked: "I've served a life sentence [fourteen years] in the Andamans for throwing a bomb at a British official. But," he added, "we don't know how to make these things as well as you British and Americans, so it didn't go off, and I was caught." I remarked that I supposed he was glad that it didn't go off.

"Yes," he said, "for it turned out to be the wrong man." And he said it as casually as if he had been talking about the weather. The cult of the bomb was respectable.

Mahatma Gandhi brought all this festering hate and intrigue to the surface. He would make the movement for independence open and frank and nonviolent. At the close of one of my "after meetings" I walked home with a seeker, a Hindu. I asked him what he was doing, and he laughed and said he belonged to the C.I.D., the secret police. He came to watch me and stayed to pray! And then he said this revealing thing:

Before Mahatma Gandhi came, everything was underground. He brought the whole thing to the surface. Now we simply go to the Congress headquarters and ask: "What are you going to do next?" And they outline their next moves in the fight with Government. And it always turns out that way. They never deceive us. It is all very easy now.

Easy? He really didn't see what was happening. He didn't see that here was a new and efficient weapon that was always striking at the heart. You didn't quite know how to counter it.

To see the power and directness and simplicity of the method of nonviolent non-co-operation let us look at Mahatma Gandhi's first trial and imprisonment before a British judge. Here was one of the most dramatic and destiny-filled scenes in history. C. F. Andrews says: "The trial itself was noteworthy, both for the dignity of the prisoner at the bar and also for the noble utterance of the judge who delivered the sentence. Much of the bitterness at the time was taken away from men's minds owing to the judge's speech." [5] Here the two systems were at their best and spoke their best in these pregnant moments. I quote the whole statement of each, for they give an insight into the struggle better than long descriptions could. The Mahatma's statement:

Before I read this statement, I would like to state that I entirely endorse the learned advocate-general's remarks in connection with my humble self. It is the most painful duty with me, but I have to discharge that duty knowing the responsibility that rests upon my shoulders, and

[5] *Mahatma Gandhi's Ideas*, p. 290.

I wish to endorse all the blame that the learned advocate-general has thrown on my shoulders in connection with the Bombay, Madras, and Chauri Chaura occurrences. Thinking over these deeply and sleeping over them, night after night, it is impossible for me to dissociate myself from the diabolical crimes of Chauri Chaura, or the mad outrages of Bombay. He is quite right when he says that, as a man of responsibility, a man having received a fair share of education, having had a fair share of experience of this world, I should have known the consequences of every one of my acts. I know that I was playing with fire. I ran the risk, and if I was set free, I would still do the same. I have felt it this morning, that I would have failed in my duty if I did not say what I said here just now.

I wanted to avoid violence; I want to avoid violence. Nonviolence is the first article of my faith. It is also the last article of my creed. But I had to make my choice. I had either to submit to a system which I considered had done an irreparable harm to my country, or incur the risk of the mad fury of my people bursting forth when they understood the truth from my lips. I know that my people have sometimes gone mad. I am deeply sorry for it, and I am therefore here to submit, not to a light penalty, but to the highest penalty. I do not ask for mercy. I do not plead any extenuating act. I am here, therefore, to invite and cheerfully submit to the highest penalty that can be inflicted upon me for what in law is a deliberate crime, and what appears to me to be the highest duty of a citizen. The only course open to you, the judge, is, as I am just going to say in my statement, either to resign your post or inflict on me the severest penalty, if you believe that the system and law you are assisting to administer are good for the people. I do not expect that kind of conversion, but by the time I have finished with my statement, you will perhaps have a glimpse of what is raging within my breast to run this maddest risk which a sane man can run.

I owe it, perhaps, to the Indian public and to the public in England that I should explain why from a staunch loyalist and co-operator I have become an uncompromising disaffectionist and non-co-operator. To the court, too, I should say why I plead guilty to the charge of promoting disaffection towards the government established by law in India.

My public life began in 1893 in South Africa in troubled weather. My first contact with British authority in that country was not of a happy character. I discovered that as a man and an Indian I had no rights. More correctly, I discovered that I had no rights as a man because I was an Indian.

But I was not baffled. I thought that this treatment of Indians was an excrescence upon a system that was intrinsically and mainly good. I gave the government my voluntary and hearty co-operation, criticizing it freely where I felt it was faulty, but never wishing its destruction.

Consequently, when the existence of the Empire was threatened in 1899 by the Boer challenge, I offered my services to it, raised a volunteer ambulance corps, and served at several actions that took place for the relief of Ladysmith. Similarly in 1906, at the time of the Zulu revolt, I raised a stretcher-bearing party and served till the end of the rebellion. On both these occasions I received medals, and was even mentioned in dispatches. For my work in South Africa, I was given by Lord Hardinge a Kaiser-i-Hind Gold Medal. When the war broken out in 1914 between England and Germany, I raised a volunteer ambulance corps in London, chiefly students. Its work was acknowledged by the authorities to be valuable. Lastly, in India, when a special appeal was made at the War Conference in Delhi in 1918 by Lord Chelmsford for recruits, I struggled at the cost of my health to raise a corps in Khaira, and the response was being made when the hostilities ceased and orders were received that no more recruits were wanted. In all these efforts at service I was actuated by the belief that it was possible by such service to gain a status of full equality in the Empire for my countrymen.

The first shock came in the shape of the Rowlatt Act, a law designed to rob the people of all real freedom. I felt called upon to lead an intensive agitation against it. Then followed the Punjab horrors, beginning with the massacre at Jallianwala Bagh and culminating in crawling orders, public floggings, and other indescribable humiliations. I discovered too that the plighted word of the Prime Minister to the Moslems of India regarding the integrity of Turkey and the holy places of Islam was not likely to be fulfilled. But in spite of forebodings and the grave warnings of friends, at the Amritsar Congress in 1919 I fought for co-operation and for working the Montagu-Chelmsford reforms, hoping that the Prime Minister would redeem his promise to the Indian Moslems, that the Punjab wound would be healed, and that the reforms, inadequate and unsatisfactory though they were, marked a new era of hope in the life of India.

But all that hope was shattered. The Khilafat promise was not to be redeemed. The Punjab crime was whitewashed; and most of the culprits went not only unpunished but remained in service, continued to draw pensions from the Indian revenues, and in some cases were even rewarded; I saw too that not only did the reforms not mark a change of heart, but they were only a method of further draining India of her wealth and of prolonging her servitude.

I came reluctantly to the conclusion that the British connection has made India more helpless than she ever was before, politically and economically. A disarmed India has no power of resistance against any aggressor if she wants to engage in an armed conflict with him. So much is this the case that some of our best men consider that India must take generations before she can achieve dominion status. She has become so poor that she has little power of resisting famines.

Before the British advent, India spun and wove in her millions of cottages just the supplement she needed for adding to her meager agricultural resources. This cottage industry, so vital for India's existence, has been ruined by incredibly heartless and inhuman processes, as described by English witnesses.

Little do town dwellers know how the semi-starved masses of India are slowly sinking to lifelessness. Little do they know that their miserable comfort represents the brokerage they get for the work they do for the foreign exploiter, that the profits and the brokerage are sucked from the masses. Little do they realize that the government established by law in British India is carried on for this exploitation of the masses. No sophistry, no jugglery in figures, can explain away the evidence that the skeletons in many villages present to the naked eye. I have no doubt whatsoever that both England and the town dwellers of India will have to answer if there is a God above for this crime against humanity, which is perhaps unequaled in history.

The law itself in this country has been used to serve the foreign exploiter. My unbiased examination of the Punjab martial law cases has led me to believe that at least 95 per cent of convictions were wholly bad. My experience of political cases in India leads me to the conclusion that in nine out of every ten the condemned men were totally innocent. Their crime consisted in their love of their country. In ninety-nine cases out of a hundred, justice has been denied to Indians as against Europeans in the courts of India.

This is not an exaggerated picture. It is the experience of almost every Indian who has had anything to do with such cases. In my opinion, the administration of the law is thus prostituted, consciously or unconsciously, for the benefit of the exploiter.

The greater misfortune is that the Englishmen and their Indian associates in the administration of the country do not know that they are engaged in the crime I have attempted to describe. I am satisfied that many Englishmen and Indian officials honestly believe that they are administering one of the best systems devised in the world, and that India is making steady though slow progress. They do not know that a subtle but effective system of terrorism, together with an organized display of force on the one hand and the deprivation of all powers of retaliation or self-defense on the other, have emasculated the people and induced in them the habit of simulation. This awful habit has added to the ignorance and the self-deception of the administrators.

Section 124, A, under which I am happily charged, is perhaps the prince among the political sections of the Indian Penal Code designed to suppress the liberty of the citizen. Affection cannot be manufactured or regulated by law. If one has no affection for a person or system, one should be free to give the fullest expression to his disaffection, so long as he does not contemplate, promote, or incite to violence. But the section under which Mr. Banker and I are charged is one under which mere promotion of dissaffection is a crime. I have studied some of the cases tried under it, and I know that some of the most loved of India's patriots have been convicted under it. I consider it a privilege, therefore, to be charged under that section.

I have endeavored to give in their briefest outline the reasons for my disaffection. I have no personal ill will against any single administrator, much less can I have any disaffection towards the King's person. But I hold it to be a virtue to be disaffected towards a government which in its totality has done more harm to India than any previous system. India is less manly under the British rule than she ever was before. Holding such a belief, I consider it to be a sin to have affection for the system. And it has been a precious privilege for me to be able to write what I have in various articles tendered in evidence against me.

In fact, I believe that I have rendered a service to India and England by showing in non-co-operation the way out of the unnatural state in which both are living. In my humble opinion, non-co-operation with evil is as much a duty as is co-operation with good. But in the past, non-co-operation has been deliberately expressed in violence to the evildoer. I am endeavoring to show to my countrymen that violent non-co-operation only multiplies evil and that, as evil can only be sustained by violence, withdrawal of support of evil requires complete abstention from violence.

Nonviolence implies voluntary submission to the penalty for non-co-operation with evil. I am here, therefore, to invite and submit cheerfully to the highest penalty that can be inflicted upon me for what in law is a deliberate crime, and what appears to me to be the highest duty of a citizen. The only course open to you, the judge, is either to resign your post and thus dissociate yourself from evil, if you feel that the law you are called upon to administer is an evil and that in reality I am innocent, or to inflict on me the severest penalty, if you believe that the system and the law you are assisting to administer are good for the people of this country and that my activity is therefore injurious to the commonweal.

Mr. Broomfield, the judge, then gave his full judgment as follows:

Mr. Gandhi, you have made my task easy in one way by pleading guilty to the charge. Nevertheless, what remains, namely, the determination of a just sentence, is perhaps as difficult a proposition as a judge in this country could have to face. The law is no respecter of persons. Nevertheless, it will be impossible to ignore the fact that you are in a different category from any person I have ever tried or am likely to have to try. It would be impossible to ignore the fact that, in the eyes of millions of your countrymen, you are a great patriot and a great leader.

Even those who differ from you in politics look upon you as a man of high ideals and of noble and of even saintly life.

I have to deal with you in one character only. It is not my duty and I do not presume to judge or criticize you in any other character. It is my duty to judge you as a man subject to the law, who by his own admission has broken the law and committed what to an ordinary man must be a grave offense against the state. I do not forget that you have constantly preached against violence and that you have on many occasions, as I am willing to believe, done much to prevent violence. But having regard to the nature of your political teaching and the nature of many of those to whom it was addressed, how you could have continued to believe that violence would not be the inevitable consequence it passes my capacity to understand.

There are probably few people in India who do not sincerely regret that you should have made it impossible for any government to leave you at liberty. But it is so. I am trying to balance what is due to you against what appears to me to be necessary to the interest of the public, and I propose in passing sentence to follow the precedent of a case, in many respects similar to this case, that was decided some twelve years ago; I mean the case against Bal Gangadhar Tilak under the same section. The sentence that was passed upon him as it finally stood was a sentence of simple imprisonment for six years. You will not consider it unreasonable, I think, that you should be classed with Mr. Tilak, i.e., a sentence of two years' simple imprisonment on each count of the charge, six years in all, which I feel it my duty to pass upon you. And I should like to say in doing so that if the course of events in India should make it possible for the government to reduce the period and release you, no one will be better pleased than I.

Gandhi said in reply:

I would say one word. Since you have done me the honor of recalling the trial of the late Lokamanya Bal Gangadhar Tilak, I just want to say that I consider it to be the proudest privilege and honor to be associated with his name. So far as the sentence itself is concerned, I certainly consider that it is as light as any judge would inflict on me; and so far as the whole proceedings are concerned, I must say that I could not have expected greater courtesy.

Since the trial of Jesus of Nazareth this was obviously the most important trial of history. And it makes you wonder who was on trial, for obviously the prisoner was judging the judge and the system he represented. And the judge felt it too. That was one of the saving things about it, for it held great promise for the future.

This going to jail on the part of the Mahatma loosed a flood of pent-up sacrifice. Tens of thousands followed him to jail in the succeeding years. The total number is estimated at 200,000. And these were the cream of the national leaders. The policy of the government was to pick off only the top leaders and send them to jail. The rank and file were not sent. You had to be in a certain position to have the privilege of going to jail. The Congress had lists of people who would take over the movement the moment the man above was sent to jail. Then he in turn would go, and so on down the line. These men who were going to jail were men who in doing so were often sacrificing their earthly all. They gave up professions and prospects and flung them all upon the altar of the freedom of their country. A man like Motilal Nehru, the father of Jawaharlal Nehru and one of the most successful lawyers in India, a man of whom it was said that he was so modernly fashionable that he sent his shirts to Paris to be laundered, threw aside practice and fashion, began to dress in homespun and to spend much of his time in jail. The mantle of the father fell upon his son, and he went even beyond his illustrious father in sacrifice and service. This was illustrated by a very poignant scene I witnessed at the height of the movement. Jawaharlal Nehru's wife, Kamala Nehru, was ill with tuberculosis at Bhowali in the Himalayas. It was decided that she should be sent to Germany for an operation upon the lungs. I asked her if her husband, who was then in the Almora jail, would accompany her to Europe. Her reply: "I would not have him go unless he should go as a free man." The government had offered him conditional freedom. He refused and said it would be unconditional or not at all. He was given forty-eight hours to be with her before she left. Her car took her down the mountain to the train and thence to the boat to Europe. His car took him back to the jail in the mountains. Neither would bend, let alone break, in that critical moment. Later the government relented and let him go unconditionally. But it was out of that stern stuff the new India was made. When Jawaharlal Nehru would be released from jail—he was sent to jail fourteen times—he would say exactly the same things which had put him there before. I would hold my breath to watch him come out of jail, say the same things, and go back again, and do it without a quiver and without a whimper. It was a training of a new kind of army, an army of nonviolent resisters. India was shedding her fears—her fears of jails, of lathee charges, of her rulers. A timid people were being forged into a very courageous and unconquerable host. When charges of the police with their long bamboo poles, called lathees, took place to break up the forbidden assemblies of the people, the resisters would stand up under the blows; and when they fell, they fell without resistance and often without hate. It was the greatest training in spirit that any nation has ever undergone.

Webb Miller, special correspondent of the *New York World-Telegram*, describes the scenes in Dharasana Camp, Surat, Bombay Presidency, during the Non-co-operation Movement of 1930:

During the morning I saw and heard hundreds of blows inflicted by the police, but not a single blow returned by the volunteers. . . . In no case did I see a volunteer even raise an arm to deflect the blows from lathees. There were no outcries from the beaten Swarajists, only groans after they had submitted to their beating. . . . In eighteen years of reporting in twenty-two countries, during which I have witnessed innumerable civil disturbances, riots, street fights, and rebellions, I have never witnessed such harrowing scenes as at Dharasana. The Western mind can grasp violence returned by violence, can understand a fight, but is, I found, perplexed and baffled by the sight of men advancing coldly and deliberately and submitting to beating without attempting defense. Sometimes the scenes were so painful that I had to turn away momentarily.

One surprising feature was the discipline of the volunteers. It seemed they were thoroughly imbued with the Gandhi's nonviolence creed, and the leaders constantly stood in front of the ranks imploring them to remember that Gandhi's soul was with them.[6]

There were breakdowns, of course. Mobs forgetting the training in nonviolence would revert to violence and bloodshed. When they did so, Gandhiji would fast against those who had strayed from the narrow way of nonviolence. And if they didn't respond, he would call off the movement. He had to fight a fight on two fronts—against the imperial power and against his own followers, who, with "*Mahatma Gandhi ki jai*" (Hail to Mahatma Gandhi) on their lips, would do violence. That he finally won out on both fronts is a tribute to the indomitable spirit of the man. When the suppression of the movement would get strongest and most apparently triumphant, then the spirit of the Mahatma arose to exultation. For he

[6] Richard B. Gregg, *The Power of Non-Violence*, pp. 35-36. Used by permission The Fellowship of Reconciliation.

had a philosophy of suffering: "They must not expect the struggle to close quickly. Time runs always in favor of the sufferer, for the simple reason that tyranny becomes more and more exposed as it is continued. In reality struggle appears to have a longer lease of life when the result is a certainty." The darkest hours would seem to be in moments when the Mahatma would call off the movement because of a departure from its spirit. Even then the Mahatma knew that he was the stronger for acknowledging his mistakes and the sins of his followers:

I am painfully conscious of my imperfections, and therein lies all the strength I possess. . . . Let the opponent glory in our humiliations and so-called defeat. It is better to be charged with cowardice than to be guilty of denial of an oath and sin against God. It is a million times better that I should be the laughingstock of the world than that I should act with insincerity towards myself. . . . I know that the drastic reversal of practically the whole of the program may be politically unsound and unwise, but there is no doubt it is religiously sound. The country will have gained by my humiliation and confession of error. I lay claim to no superhuman powers. I wear the same corruptible flesh as the weakest of my fellow beings wear, and am, therefore, as liable to err as any.

The sheer courage of acknowledging your blunders and errors while carrying on a war for freedom is breath-taking. And yet here he was profoundly right again. For he was never so tall and straight as when bent under the agony of his own mistakes. Even when he stumbled, he stumbled forward. Everything furthered him, for he was essentially honest. He was disconcertingly honest. He said everything he thought. Dr. John R. Mott once remarked, "The greatest thing you have ever done is the observance of your day of silence." Yet Gandhiji said to Louis Fischer about it:

I used to travel morning, noon, and night in hot trains, and on open bullock carts throughout hot India; and thousands of people would come to ask me questions, make pleas, and beg that I pray with them, and I used to get tired; so I introduced the weekly day of silence. Since then I have clothed this weekly day of silence in all kinds of moral virtues and given it philosophic content, but actually it was because I wanted a day off.

It is disconcerting to bare your inmost self when in quiet conversation with your friends and to strip your motives bare, but to do it while in the face of the "enemy" shows a startling bravery. To say to your "enemy," "I am weak here and there," is to court disaster by the ordinary canons. But Gandhi could say with Paul: "I . . . glory in my infirmities, . . . for when I am weak, then am I strong," and strangely enough, he was.

But Gandhiji demanded not only outward nonviolence in the face of provocation; he demanded nonviolence even in thought:

The votary must refuse to be cowed down by his superior, without being angry. He must, however, be ready to sacrifice his post, however remunerative it may be. Whilst sacrificing his all, if the votary has no sense of irritation against his employer, he has the "ahimsa" of the brave in him. I assume that a fellow passenger threatens my son with assault, and I reason with the would-be assailant who then turns upon me. If then I take his blows with grace and dignity, without harboring any ill will against him, I exhibit the "ahimsa" of the brave. . . . If I succeed in curbing my temper every time, and, though able to give blow for blow, I refrain from doing so, I shall develop the "ahimsa" of the brave which will never fail me and which will compel recognition from the most confirmed adversaries. . . . Satyagraha is always superior to armed resistance. This can only be effectively proved by demonstration, not by argument. It is the weapon that adorns the strong. It can never adorn the weak. By weak is meant the weak in mind and spirit, not in body. . . . The sword of the Satyagrahi is love and the unshakable firmness that comes from it. . . . A Satyagrahi must always be ready to die with a smile on his face, without retaliation and without rancor in his heart. Some people had come to have a wrong idea that Satyagraha meant jail-going only; perhaps facing lathee blows and nothing more. Such Satyagraha could not bring independence. To win independence they had to learn the art of dying without killing.

He goes on and lays down rules for the behavior of the Satyagrahis:

Anyone summoned to appear before a court should do so. No defense should be offered and no pleaders engaged in the matter. If a fine is imposed, with the alternative of imprisonment, imprisonment should be accepted. If only a fine is imposed, it ought not to be paid. . . . There should be no demonstrations of grief or otherwise made by the remaining Satyagrahis by reason of the arrest and imprisonment of their comrade. It cannot be too often repeated that we court imprisonment and may not complain of it when we actually receive it. When once we are imprisoned, it is our duty to conform to all prison regulations. . . .

A Satyagrahi may not resort to surreptitious practices. All that the Satyagrahis do can only and must be done openly. To evade no punishment, to accept all suffering joyfully, and to regard it as a possibility for further strengthening his soul force, is the duty of every single one of my followers.

He gathers up his ideas into fifteen commandments:

As an individual:

1. A Satyagrahi, i.e., a civil resister, will harbor no anger.
2. He will suffer the anger of the opponent.
3. In doing so he will put up with assaults from the opponent, never retaliate; but he will not submit, out of fear of punishment or the like, to any order given in anger.
4. When any person in authority seeks to arrest a civil resister, he will voluntarily submit to the arrest, and he will not resist the attachment or removal of his own property, if any, when it is sought to be confiscated by the authorities.
5. If a civil resister has any property in his possession as a trustee, he will refuse to surrender it, even though in defending it he might lose his life. He will, however, never retaliate.
6. Nonretaliation excludes swearing and cursing.
7. Therefore a civil resister will never insult his opponent, and therefore also, he may not take part in many of the newly coined cries which are contrary to the spirit of ahimsa.
8. A civil resister will not salute the Union Jack, nor will he insult it or officials, English or Indian.
9. In course of the struggle if one insults an official or commits an assault upon him, a civil resister will protect such official or officials from the insult or attack even at the risk of his life.

As a prisoner:

10. As a prisoner, a civil resister will behave courteously toward prison officials and will observe all such discipline of the prison as is not contrary to self-respect; as for instance, while he will salaam the officials in the usual manner, he will not perform any humiliating gyrations and will refuse to shout "Victory to *Sarkar* [government]," or the like. He will take cleanly cooked and cleanly served food, which is not contrary to his religion, and will refuse to take food insultingly served or served in unclean vessels.
11. A civil resister will make no distinction between an ordinary prisoner and himself, will in no way regard himself as superior to the rest; nor will he ask for any conveniences that may not be necessary for keeping his body in good health and condition. He is entitled to ask

for such conveniences as may be required for his physical and spiritual well-being.

12. A civil resister may not fast for want of conveniences whose deprivation does not involve any injury to one's self-respect.

As a unit:

13. A civil resister will joyfully obey all the orders issued by the leader of the corps, whether they please him or not.

14. He will carry out orders in the first instance even though they appear to him to be insulting, inimical, or foolish, and then appeal to higher authority. He is free to determine the fitness of the corps to satisfy him before joining it; but after he has joined it, it becomes his duty to submit to its discipline, irksome or otherwise. If the sum total of the energy for the corps appears to a member to be improper or immoral, he has a right to sever his connection; but, being within it, he has no right to commit a breach of its discipline.

15. No civil resister is to expect maintenance for his dependents. It would be an accident if any such provision was made. A civil resister entrusts his dependents to the care of God. Even in ordinary warfare wherein hundreds of thousands give themselves up to it, they are able to make no previous provision. How much more, then, should such be the case in Satyagraha? It is the universal experience that in such times hardly anybody is left to starve.

When one takes the attitude of the real Satyagrahi, it throws around him something that disarms his enemies. The Moslems of Noakhali slaughtered the Hindus in mass slaughter. The Mahatma deliberately went into these scenes of desolation and hate, and went unarmed. India held its breath. Would he too be slaughtered? He trudged from village to village, calling on the people to restore the burned houses. He himself stayed in the houses of Moslems wherever possible. The amazing courage of it! It so moved India that Mrs. Sarojini Naidu, a Hindu, exclaimed: "Like Christ of old he trudges the muddy paths of Noakhali and brings peace." A hitherto unpublished account of an incident in Noakhali was given by a highly placed newspaperman who was not allowed at the time to publish it for obvious reasons. But he now gives me permission to publish it.

When the Mahatma would trudge from village to village on his peace mission, the goondas [bad characters] would flee before him, afraid to face him. Those who did come and face him almost always were converted by the Mahatma and promised to hold themselves responsible for keeping the peace. He arranged with the government that no one should be arrested in his prayer meetings. One Moslem came and was unaffected by the Mahatma. He grabbed the Mahatma by the throat and choked him till he was blue in the face. In the midst of it the Mahatma kept on smiling and even laughing. The absence of resistance and even of resentment so unnerved the attacker that he desisted. Later he came and fell at the Mahatma's feet and begged forgiveness for what he had done. The Mahatma carried on as though nothing had happened.

One of India's greatest philosophers, Sir S. Radhakrishnan, sums up Gandhiji and his nonviolence movement:

Gandhiji embodies the wounded pride of India, and in his Satyagraha is reflected the eternal patience of her wisdom. Gandhiji admits that submission to injustice is worse than suffering it. He tells us that we can resist through an act of nonviolence, which is an active force. If blood be shed, let it be our blood. Cultivate the quiet courage of dying without killing; for man lives freely only by his readiness to die, if need be, at the hands of his brother, never by killing him. . . . When faced by crisis they would prefer the four walls of a cell to a seat in the Cabinet or a tent on the battlefield. They would be prepared to stand against a wall to be spat upon, to be stoned, to be shot. Gandhiji today is not a free man. You may crucify the body of such a man; but the light in him, which is from the divine flame of truth and love, cannot be put out.

This was written when he was in jail: "Gandhiji today is not a free man." But as we look back, we see that he was one of the freest of men—even in jail.

All of this seems idealistic and impossible. But not when you see it applied on a mass scale to a political situation. Then you see the sheer power of it, a strange new power that shakes you to your depths, and shakes a nation to its depths—the nation that adopts it and the nation against whom it is adopted. At first you are disposed to incredulity or mockery, and then something gets past your armor and gets you. I remember how I recoiled against it when it was first suggested. I wrote Mahatma Gandhi begging him not to begin nonviolent civil disobedience. I thought it too dangerous. And then came his reply:

May I assure you I shall not embark on civil disobedience without just cause, not without proper precautions and more, not without copious praying. You have, perhaps, no notion of the wrong that this government has done and is still doing to the vital part of our being. But I must not argue. I invite you to pray with and for me.

Behind the gentle words there was a determination of steel. And there was always a sense of being an instrument of something bigger than the occasion. He felt he was an instrument of God for a world situation and some day his method would be needed in world affairs. He reminds the representatives of the old political methods, who call his plans impracticable and fantastic, that

the steam engineer was laughed at by the horse dealer till he saw that even horses could be transported by the steam engine. The electrical engineer was no doubt called a faddist and a madman in steam-engine circles till work was actually done over the wires. It may be long before the law of love will be recognized in international affairs. Yet if only we watched the latest developments in Europe and Eastern Asia with an eye to essentials, we could see how the world is moving steadily to realize that between nation and nation, as between man and man, force has failed to solve problems.

Since that was written, we have seen the world situation go from bad to worse under the reign of force. It is solving nothing. It is getting us deeper and deeper into the mire. Force begets force; hate begets hate; and toughness begets a greater toughness. It is all a descending spiral, and the end is destruction—for everybody.

Gandhi has taken this method out of the realm of idealism, has applied it on a vast scale, and has demonstrated its practicability. India has won her independence, and she won it by nonviolent means. It took thirty years to win it, but the time would have been greatly shortened had not violence crept into the movement. To the degree that it has remained nonviolent it has been power—pure, unadulterated power. Its only weakness was in the departure from its own principles and practice. Had India been true to the principles and practice of the Mahatma's nonviolent movement, she would have assumed the moral leadership of the world. The violence that crept into the movement when it was on and the violence that has attended the adjustments between Pakistan and India have tended to dim that moral leadership, and yet through it all the amazing power of Mahatma Gandhi and his method shines. Nothing can dim that. Just as the spirit of Jesus shines all the more against the background of the treachery of Judas, so the spirit of Mahatma Gandhi shines all the more against the background of the betrayal of his spirit, often by those who named his name.

The method of nonviolent non-co-operation would make any nation safe, if really applied. For you cannot rule over a nation unless that nation allows you. You cannot rule over a people that simply withdraws from you and leaves you high and dry. And when you react by violence and throw people in jail, then your weapons are struck out of your hands. All you succeed in doing is not to punish the persons but to honor them. They become national heroes. That happened in India: the more people were sent to jail, the more they were esteemed. You were nobody in India if you had not been to jail! And the length of time spent in jail determined the degree of affection produced. And not only were your weapons struck out of your hands, but you were weakened the more you struck. The more physically oppressive you became, the weaker you became. And vice versa. The more the nonviolent resister for truth resists with patience, the stronger he becomes. Mahatma Gandhi and Jawaharlal Nehru were made by jail. These periods of lull between storms gave them time to reflect, to gather direction, and to write. Jawaharlal Nehru wrote his great books in jail, and they are in increasing demand today as the world gradually sees the meaning and power of this nonviolent movement. What can you do with a movement like that? The more you attempt to crush it by physical violence, the weaker you become, and the stronger they become! Another thing must be noted: "Almost every man who went to jail became spiritualized in the process. . . . Almost all of us turned to the study of religion and prayer. We came out better men than when we went in." These are the words of a disciple of the Mahatma who had spent years in jail. You shut up people in jails only to deepen their spiritual life and broaden their mental outlook and prepare them for moral and political leadership. Government jails became training schools for leadership in the new India.

Gandhiji sums up the meaning of the movement in these words:

Passive resistance is an all-sided sword; it can be used any how; it blesses him who uses it and also against whom it is used, without drawing a drop of blood. It produces far-reaching results. It never rusts, and it cannot be stolen. The sword of passive resistance does not require a scabbard, and one cannot be forcibly dispossessed of it. . . . It is quite plain that passive resistance thus understood is infinitely superior to physical force, and that it requires greater courage than the latter.

This method and this spirit have been deeply implanted into the soul of India. In many ways they are God's most precious deposit in a world about to ruin itself by physical force. This method has been demonstrated on a vast scale, and the results have been amazing, almost beyond belief. People who were cooped up in jails for years now ruling the destinies of 300,000,000 people! Last year in Travancore state force was riding high, and tyranny supreme, and the state Congress leaders expelled from the state or in jail. This year those same men are running the state, and the center of that tyranny, Sir C. P. Ramaswami Aiyar, the prime minister, has left in disgrace. His regime of tyranny went down like a house of cards, defeated by its own methods.

There are perhaps many Western Christians who cannot get at the truth in the Mahatma because it is wrapped in strange Eastern and Hindu forms. But those forms are not of the essence of things. It is the thing itself that matters. Here was a man who applied on a national scale the truth that we Christians see in the Cross. There is much more in the Cross than Mahatma Gandhi applied— God seeking us redemptively, bearing in his own body our sins, and stretching out his arms from a cross welcoming a penitent humanity. We see this and more at the Cross. But never in human history has so much light been shed on the Cross as has been through this one man, and that man not even called a Christian. Had not our Christianity been so vitiated and overlain by our identification with unchristian attitudes and policies in public and private life, we would have seen at once the kinship between Gandhi's method and the Cross. Non-Christians saw it instinctively.

Vallabhai Patel, the home minister, said to me in the early days of the Gandhian movement, "It is you Christians who can understand our movement better than anyone else," for he saw it had a kinship with the Cross. A Hindu non-co-operator who had been in jail said to me years ago, "We know now what you Christians are talking about when you talk about the Cross, for we are taking it." That had in it an unconscious barb—you talk about the cross; we take it! A Christian judge said to me in the days when men were going to jail in droves: "They are more Christian than I am, though they are nearly all Hindus. They can take only a very limited number of things into jail with them, and, as I have to approve what they take, I find that nearly all ask to take the New Testament with them." Many of them in being sentenced by a Christian judge would say as they left the courtroom: "Father, forgive them; for they know not what they do." In one place, Patna, it was Easter, and the Hindu leader of the movement sent a note to the British superintendent of police saying: "Today is Easter, and you will probably want to go to church, so we are not sending the usual batch of volunteers to be arrested." A gentle hint! In another place where the volunteers were arrested as soon as they crossed a certain fixed point, word was sent to the magistrate who gave the order for arrest: "It is hot, and we do not want to give you unnecessary trouble during the heat of the day, so we will not send the volunteers until evening time. Please be ready to arrest fifty at five o'clock." So permeated with the Christian spirit did the movement become that the Bishop of Madras, an Englishman, said in a public address: "I frankly confess, although it deeply grieves me to say it, that I see in Mr. Gandhi, the patient sufferer for the cause of righteousness and mercy, a truer representative of the crucified Saviour than the men who have thrown him into prison and yet call themselves by the name of Christ." Lionel Fielden wrote: "How strange it seems that Christians, and in particular Christian ministers, serving in their churches and repeating the words 'Blessed are the peace-makers: for they shall be called the children of God,' can view with indifference and even approval the incarceration of Gandhi by the Pilates of today." Rufus Jones said: "I also discovered that Gandhi knew very little about another man whom he very much resembled in spirit, John Woolman, the most remarkable and the most saintly of all the Quakers of the eighteenth century and a striking example of 'soul force.' " Always in dealing with Gandhi and his movement the mind would instinctively turn to the Christian spirit of it. A Hindu follower of Gandhiji said to me one day in reference to a Moslem: "I'm afraid I didn't feel very Christian toward him." A Hindu talks about not feeling Christian toward a Mohammedan! Mixed, but illuminating! A Hindu premier of one of the provinces of India, one of the finest followers of the Mahatma, said to a Hindu doctor after going through a leper asylum: "I congratulate you. You are doing a real bit of Christian service here." This same premier said to me: "We will need all the help we can get from the West in the making of the New India, provided they come in the spirit of Christ. If they come in the spirit of Christ, they can come by the boat load." It was the Gandhi movement that made them see and appreciate the spirit of Christ. A movement that was fighting the West was showing to the West its own Saviour in a new way.

A Hindu summed it up to me in these words: "We Hindus and you Christians should change sacred books. The Bhagavad-Gita gives philosophic reasons for war, while the New Testament teaches peace, and yet we are more peace-minded and you are more war-minded. If we changed sacred books, it would suit us both better." It was said only half-seriously, but it had a sting in it.

So East and West are drawn to Gandhi. The Hindu strains in Gandhi appeal to the Hindu, and the Christian strains appeal to the Christian. Has God been preparing a man who by his background and training and spirit would appeal to both East and West? And has God let him go through the tragic death, summing up in his death what he lived for in life, and has God dramatically called through that death to the nations arming and getting ready for another conflict—called them to a way out of war? Is Gandhi God's eleventh-hour call to the nations drifting to their doom?

CHAPTER VIII

The Fastings of the Mahatma

ONE of the most difficult things for the Western mind to understand about the Mahatma was his philosophy of fasting. Lord Linlithgow wrote to the Mahatma: "I regard the use of a fast for political purposes as a form of political blackmail [himsa] for which there can be no moral justification." Many others felt it was a form of coercion. But to the Mahatma it was part and parcel of his philosophy of truth and nonviolence. For a long time even some of his colleagues thought it an eccentric and whimsical notion of the Mahatma. It is only now that the amazing moral power wrapped up in it is beginning to dawn upon our minds. It is a dangerous weapon, as the Mahatma recognized, for its blade is sharp, and he warned against its indiscriminate use. But when rightly used, it has an amazing power, as the Mahatma proved. For through his fasts the Mahatma accomplished almost as much as through his nonviolent passive resistance.

Mahatma Gandhi was an activist—a moral and spiritual activist. And fasting was one of his strategies of activism, in many ways his most powerful. To go to jail on a mass scale was a part of that activism. It brought to bear a moral force upon the heart and conscience of the authorities who jailed them. The sight of vast numbers of obviously decent citizens going to jail for a principle and for a cause is a very moving and morally searching thing. What makes them do it? What is the matter with things when men and women are willing to go to jail en masse in this quiet but dramatic fashion? What's it all about? It is a moral judgment day on the persons and the system against which it is used. But fasting goes deeper still and is used by one person to call attention to and to appeal against certain things considered morally wrong and intolerable. This focuses the moral issue, centers it in the suffering of one person, and makes one act and act quickly lest the sufferer die.

To get at the core of the matter let us be reminded that fasting can be of four types:

1. *An occasional fast to relieve an overworked digestive system.* This is physically cleansing. Someone has said, "We live off half we eat, and the doctors live off the other half." There is only one sure way to reduce, and that is to reduce the amount we eat. Fasting is an obvious and simple way of getting to that end. It is physically beneficial.

2. *Fasting as a means of personal spiritual discipline.* Mahatma Gandhi used this again and again for his own sake, for self-purification. When he felt that he was not an adequate instrument of the Divine, he undertook a fast to bring himself back to a more complete alignment. For instance, he fasted for twenty-one days because of the Hindu-Moslem tensions and riots. He did not fast against those riots, but against himself because he was not strong enough to stop those riots and tensions. He said:

I launched non-co-operation. Today I find that people are non-co-operating against one another, without any regard for nonviolence. What is the reason? Only this, that I myself am not completely nonviolent. If I were practicing nonviolence to perfection, I should not have seen the violence I see around me today. My fast is therefore a penance. I blame no one. I blame only myself. I have lost the power wherewith to appeal to people. Defeated and helpless, I must submit my petition to His Court. Only He will listen, no one else.

This is fasting for self-purification, to become a better instrument of the Divine.

3. *Fasting where one is absorbed in a moral and spiritual issue.* For the time being hunger is in abeyance as the soul fights its way through to conclusions. This was the fast of Jesus for forty days in the wilderness. The great issue of how the Kingdom of God was to come had to be fought out, and for forty days he weighed this issue, weighed that, and came to his conclusions. "And he ate nothing in those days; and when they were ended, he was hungry" (Luke 4:2 Revised Standard Version). Hunger asserted itself when the moral issue was decided. That is fasting by moral and spiritual preoccupation.

4. *Fasting to change the moral and spiritual attitudes of the one or ones against whom you are fasting.* But that is not a fair statement of this kind of fasting, for it sounds belligerent and harsh. Rather it is taking on yourself suffering, hoping that the appeal

of this suffering will be used to change the moral attitudes of the one you love in spite of what he is doing. Says Jag Parvesh Chader:

But what should a nonviolent person do when he finds his friends, relations, or countrymen refuse to give up an immoral way of life, and all arguments prove futile to evoke any response? An Ahimsa-ite must not use a semblance of force to convert the wrongdoer. He even eschews the use of any harsh language. The first step is gentle and affectionate persuasion. When it fails to produce any salutary effect, voluntarily he invites suffering in his own body to open the eyes of the person who is determined to see no light.

It is an intense moral appeal, re-enforced by his own willingness to suffer.

When Mahatma Gandhi was in the Yeravda jail, I raised this question with him as he sat on a cot in the open courtyard: "Isn't your fasting a species of coercion?"

"Yes," he said very slowly, "the same kind of coercion which Jesus exercises upon you from the cross."

I was silent. It was so obviously true that I am silent again every time I think of it. He was profoundly right. The years have clarified it. And I now see it for what it is: a very morally potent and redemptive power if used rightly. But it has to be used rightly. It is not for indiscriminate use.

When the Mahatma would advise against others using the fast, my first reaction was: "Oh, he's pre-empting the field, so he alone can stand out as morally unique and superior." It was an unkind thought, I know. I was wrong. He warned against the indiscriminate use of fasting, for he knew that to have any appeal one must have earned the right to fast by proving one's moral soundness and affection by the life he has lived and the service he has rendered. The Mahatma couldn't say that, so his pre-emptory advice against others fasting seemed that he wanted the field. It was not so. Then again he warned that "in the very nature of things fasting for any selfish gain puts itself out of court. The Satyagrahi must not fast to get himself released from jail, or have other benefits conferred upon him while in jail." There seems one exception to this when the Mahatma fasted while he was in prison to get certain rights restored to him which he had in a previous imprisonment, namely, the right to edit the *Harijan* and to carry on his work while in jail in behalf of the depressed classes. But this wasn't a personal privilege he was fasting for. It was a privilege of service to the underprivileged.

When we analyze his fasts, they were disinterested and redemptive. He says, "At a very early age I began fasting for self-purification, and then I took a prolonged fast for an erring daughter of a very dear friend." The first public fast undertaken by the Mahatma was in South Africa in connection with the indentured laborers who had joined the Satyagraha struggle. His first fast in India was undertaken in 1918 in connection with the Ahmadabad millworkers' strike. After Gandhiji had fasted for three days, the mill owners and workers came to a settlement. (Incidentally, the relationships between the mill owners and workers at Ahmadabad are the best in India, and the reason is that both sides have been deeply influenced by the spirit of the Mahatma, whose Ashram was situated on the opposite bank of the river.) The next fast was a fast undertaken by the Mahatma as a penance for the Chauri Chaura tragedy of 1922 when twenty-one policemen were killed by a mob. In September, 1924, after the Kohat riots, the Mahatma undertook a fast for twenty-one days at the house of Maulana Mohammed Ali "as an effective prayer both to Hindus and Moslems not to commit suicide." Then followed in 1932 a fast unto death as a protest against the Communal Award. This Communal Award was given by the Ramsay MacDonald government to the untouchables in the form of a separate electorate. This would mean, said the Mahatma, that the untouchables would forever remain untouchables, for their status is fixed by a separate electorate. He wanted to wipe out untouchability. He also protested against this bisection of the Hindus by setting the untouchables off into a separate electorate. He was profoundly right—subsequent events have proved it. The fast was broken on the twenty-sixth day with the signing of the Poona Pact, in which the Hindus themselves gave the untouchables a high proportion of seats in the legislatures without a separate electorate. In the same year the Mahatma undertook a sympathetic fast with Apa Patwardhan, whose request to do scavenger's work in jail had been refused by the authorities. Hindus fasting for the privilege of doing scavenger's work, the cleaning of the latrines! After they had fasted two days, the authorities granted the necessary permission. In May, 1933, he undertook a fast of twenty-one days for the purification of himself and his associates. This was followed by a short fast in 1934 as a penance for an assault on a Sanatanist (orthodox Hindu) by a social reformer. In 1939 the Mahatma commenced a fast unto death in connection with the happenings in the native state of Rajkot, his own state. The viceroy's intervention led to a settlement and the termination of the fast. On February 10, 1943, Gandhiji, while a prisoner in the palace of the Aga Khan, the spiritual head of the Moslem Khoja community, undertook a fast of three weeks as the government fastened on him and his associates the responsibility for the August, 1942, riots and general destruction and disorder. The viceroy said Gandhi was responsible, and Gandhi charged that the wholesale arrests of the national leaders and the refusal of the viceroy to see him and try to come to a settlement were responsible. When he began the fast, the government offered to release him lest he die on their hands.

Three fasts I mention separately. One was the fast in the Sabarmati Ashram in December, 1925. Two boys were guilty of immorality in the Ashram. He fasted for seven days. At the close of the fast he said to the boys:

Why did I take that step? There were three ways open to me: (1) Punishment. I could follow the easy road of corporal punishment. As a teacher I had no option but to reject this accepted method, for I know by experience that it is futile and even harmful. (2) Indifference. I could have left you to your fate. This indifference did not appeal to me. (3) The third was the method of Love. Your character is to me a sacred trust. I must therefore try to enter into your lives, your innermost thoughts, your desires, and your impulses, and help you to eradicate impurities, if any. I discovered irregularities among you. What was I to do? Punishing you was out of the question. Being the chief among the teachers, I had to take the punishment on myself in the form of fasting which breaks today. I have learned a lot during these days of quiet thinking. What have you? Could you assure me that you will never repeat your mistake?

To those brokenhearted boys he offered forgiveness and a restoration of fellowship. But it was not a cheap forgiveness, based upon his authority as the head of the institution. It was a forgiveness that had the stain of his own blood upon it. Since he had taken their sins into his own heart and had suffered, he could now offer a forgiveness that was an expiation and an appeal. On this he comments:

If I am to identify myself with the grief of the least in India, aye, if I have the power, the least in the world, let me identify myself with the sins of the little ones who are under my care. And so doing in all humility I hope some day to see God—Truth—face to face.

He was never more Christlike than in those seven days of identifying himself with the sins of the little ones under his care. Identifying himself with the sins of the little ones under his care—that is the meaning of the Cross. That is what God did: "God was in Christ, reconciling the world unto himself." To reconcile he had to bear our own sins in his own body on a tree. That is the supreme identification—identification at the place of our sin. And we cannot be too grateful to the Mahatma for illuminating the Cross for us. No wonder the Hindu editor of the *Indian Social Reformer* exclaimed: "The Mahatma in jail has achieved in a short while what Christian missions with all their resources of men and money have not done in one hundred years. He has turned India's face to Christ and the Cross." [1] That leaves a sting, but a healing sting, for we are grateful that the face of a people was turned toward Christ and the Cross, even though we were not the agents. Perhaps "when the mists have rolled away," and understanding is not clouded by outgrown clashes, we shall see that after all the patient work of humble missionaries has laid the foundations—some of them, at least—for this turning of the face of the people to the Cross.

There is another fast that needs to be looked at, for to me it is one of the most astonishing of all—the fast over the Rajkot situation. The Mahatma fasted that democratic reforms might be put in the state. In the middle of the fast he appealed to the viceroy, who intervened, and the chief justice gave an award which conceded what the Mahatma wanted in the way of democratic reforms. The fast seemed a success. The *London News Chronicle* described the settlement as "not merely a personal triumph, but a remarkable victory for the method of passive resistance." It was a success—to everybody except the Mahatma. His very sensitive moral nature began to see that he had mixed up his methods. He had fasted—that was a moral appeal to the Ruler. And he had appealed to the viceroy, who gave a settlement—that was a legal way out. He had mixed his methods. This, the prime minister of Rajkot said, constituted a threat: "You are still hanging the award over my head." So the Mahatma renounced the award, apologizing to the viceroy and the

[1] May, 1922.

chief justice for the needless trouble he had given them. He appealed to the prime minister to come to terms with the people as if the award were not in existence.

I recognize my error. At the end of my fast I had permitted myself to say that it had succeeded as no previous fast had done. I now see it was tainted with himsa, or coercion. My fast to be pure should have been addressed only to the *Takore Sahib* [the Ruler], and I should have been content to die if I could not have melted his heart.

Concerning the effect of this rightabout-face on his co-workers he says:

Many of them are filled with misgivings. My exposition of ahimsa is new to them. They see no cause for my repentance. They think that I am giving up a great chance created by the award. . . . I have told them that their fears are unjustified, and that every act of purification, every accession of courage, adds to the strength of the cause of the people.

Gandhiji's aged sister was perturbed when she heard that he had been defeated. "Tell sister," said Gandhiji, "there is no defeat in the confession of one's error. The confession itself is a victory." He says in conclusion:

Only trust can beget trust. I lacked it myself. But at last I have regained my lost courage. My faith in the sovereign efficiency of ahimsa burns brighter for my confessions and repentances.[2]

What are we to think of a man who, at the end of a great period of suffering and triumph through that suffering, renounces his victory because the means of attaining it were tainted? An English paper said: "His passive methods are an interesting contrast to power politics." In power politics you gain your ends of power with any means at your disposal. But the uniqueness of Gandhi was in this: he was more concerned with means than with ends. He knew that if you kept to right means, you would come out to right ends. A big business executive in America is going about speaking to service clubs: "Do the right thing, and right results will follow. The moral universe guarantees it." But the Mahatma not only preached it; he practiced it, and practiced it at the moment of seem-

Harijan, May 17, 1939.

ing victory. This is so morally refreshing that it makes you feel as though you've had a soul bath.

I sit here by the window in this Indian city, and in front of me rise the high, forbidding walls of a jail. Police guards parade night and day. Inside is an attempt to make men good by coercion. It is a failure—an expensive failure—for 75 per cent of the prisoners who go out come back again. It is not redemptive. They try to make people good by giving suffering. The Mahatma made people good by taking suffering. And yet we who are practicing coercion in every phase of our civilization pretend to be shocked at the Mahatma's practice of coercion through fasting. It is a coercion, just as God coerces us by setting us in a world of moral law where we get hurt if we disobey, but it is a redemptive coercion. So Gandhi's fasts were redemptive. Not one of the fasts was to gain a personal or selfish end. They were always harnessed to the good of others. They were morally creative.

The one place where there is a question is the fast which Lord Linlithgow, the viceroy, called "political blackmail" and himsa—the fast over who was responsible for the August, 1942, riots. Concerning this the Mahatma says:

Despite your description of it as "a form of political blackmail," it is on my part meant to be an appeal to the Highest Tribunal for justice which I have failed to secure from you. If I do not survive the ordeal, I shall go to the Judgment Seat with the fullest faith in my innocence. Posterity will judge between you as the representative of an all-powerful government and me as a humble man who has tried to serve his country and humanity through it.[8]

If one looks on the Indian struggle for independence as a purely political struggle, then to use fasting to gain a political advantage is questionable, and worse, it is wrong. But if one looks on the struggle as a great moral and spiritual struggle, as the Mahatma did, then to use such means was not only proper, but highly commendable and cleansing. For the first time in human history a nation in the attainment of its national ends has repudiated force and has substituted the power of its own suffering. That is unique.

And the one who takes the method wins even if he loses. If there is no effect on the other, then it comes back to you. You are en-

[8] Letter, Feb. 7, 1943.

nobled by the very nobility of your means. Jesus said, "Whatever house you enter, first say, 'Peace be to this house!' And if a son of peace is there, your peace shall rest upon him; but if not, it shall return to you" (Luke 10:5-6 Revised Standard Version). If the other man receives your peace, well and good; but if he doesn't, then your peace returns to you. You are more peaceful for having given it. So Mahatma Gandhi jokingly said as he went through one of his fasts, "Heads I win, and tails I also win." There was a profound philosophy in that joke. Since we are born of the qualities which we habitually give out, then if we give out love, we become a loving person; if we give out hate, we become a hateful person. The Mahatma through his fasts was giving out redemptive good will and in the process became just what he was: a man of good will—a Mahatma, a great-souled man.

But the two fasts which were the last and crowning acts of his life were the most telling in their effects and the most conclusive as to the method. In both places, Calcutta and Delhi, he wrought miracles. I was in both places just before the fasts. From my room in Calcutta I could look down on streets that had been strewn with the dead. The city was festering with hate, left over from the riots. Periodically the riots were renewed. So the Mahatma knew that Calcutta was a decisive battleground. The future of the new India was bound up in this, its largest city.

Gandhiji stayed at a Moslem home in the very center of the riot district. Suhrawardy, the Moslem ex-premier, called by the Hindus "The Butcher" because of his supposed encouraging of the riots, now changed, came to stay with the Mahatma. The crowds stoned the place, partly because of the presence of Suhrawardy and partly because the Mahatma did not go where the Hindus had been sinned against. In the midst of the stoning the Mahatma walked out and said to the crowd, "Carry out my dead body, but I will not leave." A stone aimed at the Mahatma was caught by a police officer who cried out, "Kill me, not him." It was arranged that deputations should come and lay their grievances before the Mahatma. One deputation of hotheaded youths came, sure they could worst the Mahatma in argument. They came away subdued and converted. "The Mahatma is right," was all they could say. When asked about the arguments he used, they could only repeat, "The Mahatma is right." Thus a number of deputations of young men came with the same result. They were converted. They brought in a bandaged Hindu to convince the Mahatma of the brutalities they had suffered. The Mahatma took off the bandages and found the man was whole. He had been bandaged for the occasion! The Mahatma's uncanny insight and goodness were stripping off their veneer of argument and literally exposing their hypocrisy. But this was getting nowhere. So the Mahatma decided to fast to death unless they changed. It was a real gamble with his life. At the end of seventy-two hours both sides came and agreed to guarantee with their lives the lives of the opposite community—this from the governor down. More astonishing still was the fact that the people brought weapons used in the riots—from knives to Sten guns—and laid them at the Mahatma's feet. The atmosphere changed overnight. Peace crept into the hearts of the embittered people. Lord Mountbatten, a military man himself, said in relation to the miracle that had happened: "What 50,000 well-equipped soldiers could not do, the Mahatma has done. He has brought peace. He is a one-man boundary force." And it has lasted. Nearly two years have gone by, and Calcutta has been at peace, conquered by the spiritual power of the Mahatma.

The battle of Calcutta was great; the battle of Delhi was greater. When I landed in Delhi in January, 1948, the first words spoken to me were: "You're in the midst of a civil war." There were no signs of fighting, but the tensions were great. The city was the nerve center of the communal problems of India. It was a depression-laden and a hate-laden atmosphere. Gandhiji knew that he would have to clean this cesspool of hate, or it would poison the entire body of India. Just as he had advised the Graduates Association, "Be scavengers," so he was now to be a scavenger to clean up the capital of India. He must "do or die" at Delhi. It turned out to be both. He drew up eight points on which Hindus and Moslems must come to agreement or he would fast unto death. All the eight points were in favor of the Moslems. They were as follows:

1. The annual fair at the mausoleum of Khwaja Bakhtiyar, which falls due shortly, may be held, and Moslems may be able to join it without any fear.

2. The 117 mosques which after recent riots in Delhi were converted into temples or residential places may be turned into mosques again by non-Moslems of particular areas.

3. Moslems should be able to move about freely and without any danger in Karolbagh, Subzi Mandi, and Paharganj, which formerly were predominantly Moslem areas.

4. Hindus should not object to the return to Delhi of those Moslems who have perforce gone to Pakistan, if and when they choose to return.

5. Moslems should be able to travel in railway trains without any risk.

6. There should be no economic boycott of Moslems.

7. Accommodation of non-Moslems in Moslem zones in Delhi must be left entirely at the discretion of residents of those areas.

8. The fifty-five crores (550,000,000) of rupees due to Pakistan should be paid.

The sheer courage of fasting on eight points, all in favor of the Moslems and all laying on Hindus definite obligations, is breathtaking. And remember: he staked his life on their fulfillment. If there was ever a gamble for peace, here was one! What if the Hindus should refuse or hesitate? He never considered that. He considered one thing: Are my method and my aim right? If so, then the consequences are in the hands of God. His method and his aim were right, and he went as straight as an arrow to the heart of a nation. He shook that nation to its depths—shook it morally. When the representatives of the various communities gathered on the sixth day and signed the Pact of Peace, this was no cheap signing of an ordinary peace pact. There was a moral quality here that made it different. His blood and their tears cemented the pact. And it has been kept, not merely in the letter of the law, but in the spirit. A new spirit has gripped India. Now there is peace. You feel it; you know it—this is not a mere truce. There is the feel of the real upon it.

And what armed forces, exerting all the physical pressure they could; and what conferences, exerting all the pressure of sensible agreement; and what all the speeches, exerting the pressure of persuasive words—what all these could not do, Mahatma Gandhi did by his two fasts: he brought peace. And he brought peace, not at the margins, but at the centers—Calcutta and Delhi. The battle for the New India had to be fought out at those two places—one near the border of East Pakistan and the other near the border of West Pakistan. They were the centers of the problems of the new India. The Grand Old Warrior for peace fought his two greatest battles at the very end of his career at the age of seventy-nine. He could say with another Grand Old Warrior: "I have fought a good fight, I have finished my course." These were the two crowning acts of his life.

There was nothing left now for him to do, except to die as a martyr for the things for which he lived. His martyrdom crowned and sealed the whole struggle of his life. Evil, which he had fought throughout his long life, never did him a better turn than when it made him a martyr for the very things for which he lived. In the end he made evil his servant. That is mastery; that is power.

From the window where I sit writing in Bellary, India, I can see a prison and a hill fort. This hill fort crowns the summit of a rocky slope. It depicts the history of the long years of struggle for supremacy in India. A Hindu raja held it first, and, as he was being besieged by another Hindu raja, he appealed to Hyder Ali, the Moslem conqueror, to come and help him. He came by forced marches, raised the siege, and went in and took possession—for himself. French engineers helped him strengthen the fort. Then the British came and, at the defeat of Hyder Ali and Tippoo Sultan, took possession of the fort. During the world war a huge "V" was painted on the fort wall so all the city below could see it, symbol of their faith in the might of the Allies. And now the "V" has been painted out, and the tri-colored flag with the Asoka wheel at the center, the flag of the new India, Gandhi's India, is painted there instead. Military powers have come and gone, each canceling the other out, and being canceled out in turn. And at the end the flag of independence gained by nonviolent means is painted on dead forts. Is this a prophecy? Is the strongest power, and the power that will ultimately survive, the power of truth and nonviolence and capacity to suffer for a cause?

Strangely enough, the two questions of truth and nonviolence were raised at the cross. When Peter took the sword to defend him, Jesus said, "Put your sword back into its place, for all who take the sword will perish by the sword" (Revised Standard Version). Note the "all"—no exception. Has history been one long painful corroboration of that? It has, and without exception. Here was the issue of nonviolence.

Then the question of truth came up when Jesus said, "I have come into the world to bear witness to the truth. Every one who is of the truth hears my voice" (Revised Standard Version). Pilate sneeringly said, "What is truth?" He was interested only in power, military power, not in truth. So he dismissed the idea of truth and crucified the Man who witnessed to it—witnessed to it in everything he thought and said and did and was. The nonviolent Witnesser to truth was buried. Buried? Alive he walks the earth amid the ruins of kingdoms founded on blood and fear, including Pilate's kingdom, and again he weeps over them, for they are marked for doom—self-doomed. The old ways have broken down and are breaking down. Have we learned our lesson yet? God has two hands, the hand of grace and the hand of judgment. If we won't take from the hand of grace, we have to take from the hand of judgment. Must we again take from the hand of judgment, the hard way? Is Gandhi our last warning and our last call?

Gandhi is calling the world back to the Cross. It was no mere whim that made a daily paper edited and owned by non-Christians, *The Pioneer,* put out a cartoon after the Delhi fast depicting Gandhiji with a Hindu and a Moslem on each knee and at the back a cross towering over all and a rainbow behind that. They saw he was applying the Cross to modern problems. In the Moslem city of Hyderabad the death of Mahatma Gandhi was celebrated by a procession carrying his garlanded picture with a cross above it, put there by Hindus and Moslems. They saw some connection. And they saw the power of that cross.

This power works wherever it is tried, whether in a Mahatma or in a mediocre. An Indian girl, brilliant and talented, went to the West and in getting her education got something more, the habit of drink. Everything was tried to reform her. No avail. Then her father, a doctor, a disciple of the Mahatma, began to fast until she changed. She did. And she has remained free. She said to a friend of mine: "Someone had to suffer to redeem me." Here is a method which, when used by those who by their lives have earned the right to use it, is a potent power for redeeming loved ones. It can be used universally, if used wisely.

In one of my meetings during the heydey of the dictators someone arose and quoted these lines which brought a laugh:

> De Valera with his green shirts,
>   His back to the wall;
> Hitler with his brown shirts,
>   Riding for a fall;
> Mussolini with his black shirts,
>   Lording it over all;
> Three cheers for Mahatma Gandhi,
>   With no shirt at all.

It did bring a laugh, for they were the days when Mahatma Gandhi was a semijoke with the people of the West. Again and again I would have to say to my audiences: "Don't laugh at Gandhi. He will be the father of his country, just as Washington is the father of our country." I thought I was paying high tribute in saying that. Little did I know that Gandhi would be the father of his country and very much more. He will probably be the father of a new era in humanity. For note what has happened in these short years. When those lines were quoted, the men of might were in the saddle and riding human events, firmly fixed. But in a few swift years they are all three gone—Mussolini and Hitler to ignominious death amid the rubble of the empires they built up. De Valera lasted longest, for he was the mildest, but he too is gone from power. Only Gandhi remains. He has won the freedom of his country, and it is firmly established, and he is firmly established as the father of his country. And more, he has become a world issue. In a recent public meeting the presiding officer, a British judge, said: "Nothing has shaken the world like the death of Mahatma Gandhi. I haven't been the same man since." I had to arise and say: "And I haven't been the same man since." Something has happened. What is it? Why should the death of a little man shake us and the world like this—shake us who have gone through world-shaking events for years without a quiver? What has happened? Before we try to answer that, we must look at India again; then we can draw the final lesson of Gandhi's life and death.

CHAPTER IX

Sevagram Versus Delhi

NOW that the battle of independence has been won, and the battle of communal unity is on its way to being won, and the battle of unity between the native states and India is also largely won, a new battle looms as perhaps the biggest struggle of all—Sevagram versus Delhi.

This new India has inherited its soul from Mahatma Gandhi, and its symbol is Sevagram; and it has inherited its body from British imperialism, and its symbol is Delhi. The conflict between the two has begun to show itself and will probably occupy the future.

Mahatma Gandhi fought two great battles—the battle of independence and the battle of India's inner unity. Leaving the Sabarmati Ashram, he fought the battle of the independence of India for eighteen years; and then leaving Sevagram Ashram, he fought the battle of the inner unity of India for eighteen months. He never came back to Sabarmati during those eighteen years, and he never came back to Sevagram during those eighteen months. They were the centers of quiet where he gathered strength to go forth to win two of the greatest battles of history—to win them in a new way with new weapons. These two places are shrines of quiet and centers of power.

Sevagram is a village Mahatma Gandhi created five miles beyond Wardha, which at first was his headquarters. But Wardha was too much of an urban center; too many people disturbed him there, and he was not at one with his village people. So he moved out five miles with no road between; all visitors had to walk out to see him. But the P.W.D. (Permament Works Department of the government) projected a road out to his village. That began the invasion of the modern world into Sevagram. Sevagram represents the body of Mahatma Gandhi; it is the outer expression of his inner life. Geographically it is about the center of India; spiritually it was and is the center of the new India. I say "is," but that remains to be seen. For the issue is yet to be decided. In a bamboo thatched hut which was plastered with mud sat the Mahatma, and from there he ruled India. He ruled India, though he didn't hold an office. He ruled it by spiritual power. The room has been left just as he left it. He sat upon a mattress which was also his bed, covered by the white home-spun khaddar. Not a thing around him was superfluous. It met a need, or it did not stay. Anything given to him was retained if it met a need; if not, it was given to the needs of others. And the test was very severe. Two stalls were on each side of him, where two secre-taries silently worked. There were no doors within the house, save one leading to the bathroom, no chairs. When visitors came, they too sat on the floor. On the wall behind where he sat, wrought in mud is the mystic word *Om*, which stands for God, put there by a Western disciple, Miss Slade, daughter of a British admiral. On an-other wall was a card with these lines from Ruskin: "The essence of lying is in deception, not in words; a lie may be told by silence, by equivocation, by the accent on a syllable, by a glance of the eyes attaching a peculiar significance to a sentence; and all these kinds of lies are worse and baser by many degrees than a lie plainly worded." The placing of that statement on the wall is significant. He trans-ferred that to politics, put it at the center of the life of the country. I saw a banner hanging from the ceiling of the great pandal in which the Indian National Congress was being held at Cawnpore: " 'Be Honest,' Gandhi." To drop that into the center of a nation's political life is a great achievement. It was at the center of Sevagram, and he put it at the center of a nation's consciousness. To put truth and honesty into a nation's consciousness meant self-suffering. So be-side this statement on truth there was a picture of Christ kneeling in Gethsemane. In a little vestibule corner were some wooden pack-ing boxes, the only wardrobe of an Indian princess, Rajkumari Am-rit Kaur, a Christian secretary. The septic tank and the toilet were installed by a Christian missionary, Fred Williams. On the mattress on which the Mahatma sat now lie a rosary of tulsi beads, symbol of his prayer life, and beside it a twist of yarn, symbol of his love for the poor and his endeavors for their economic uplift. Religion and economics lie side by side upon his bed. Never did a soul and a body fit each other so well as this room fitted the Mahatma—every-thing simple, nothing superfluous, everything efficient. For the Ma-hatma was the soul of efficiency. He answered letters immediately; everything was done on time. Nothing sloppy or dirty or at loose ends. When a visitor's time was up, the watch was courteously shown.

An amazing amount of work was quietly done. Here momentous decisions were made. The Christian head of the Training Center for Basic Education, Aryanaikam, turned to me and in a gentle voice said, "This was the throne of India." We sat in silent meditation for about ten minutes. As we arose, we knew that this is still the throne of India—a disputed throne, but still the throne.

The living spirit of the new India is here. That spirit, embodied in Mahatma Gandhi, stands for four things: sincerity, simplicity, self-suffering, soul force. The first is sincerity—identification with truth; the second, simplicity—identification with the poor; the third, self-suffering—identification with the sins of others and taking on oneself suffering to change them; fourth, soul force—identification with the sum total of Reality and having invincible soul force as a consequence. That is what Sevagram symbolizes—and more, embodied.

Delhi, the body which the new India inherited when the British left, stands for a capital which is probably the most ornate of the world. Here the modern world and its ways are embodied. There are four things embodied here: diplomacy, bureaucracy, law and order, physical force. Instead of Sevagram's sincerity we have diplomacy; instead of simplicity we have bureaucracy; instead of self-suffering when others go wrong we have an infliction of penalty on the wrongdoer through law and order; and instead of soul force we have the physical force of a modern nation with its reliance on military power. The antithesis seems complete. But not quite. There is often sincerity in diplomacy, and here and there in Delhi are patches of simplicity amid bureaucracy. Otherwise the antithesis is complete. The question is: Which will rule the future, Sevagram or Delhi? A follower of Gandhi remarked at Sevagram, "We must choose. It is Mammon or God," and to him Delhi was Mammon, and Sevagram was God. That needs modification, of course, for God can invade Delhi, and Mammon can invade Sevagram. We can have the spirit of either in either place. But there is a real conflict.

This conflict came to tragic epitome when Jawaharlal Nehru visited a few weeks ago that little room at Sevagram and shook with unashamed emotion as he stood beside the place where the Mahatma had lived and worked—and ruled. He was a terribly lonely man without his guru. But loneliness was not the only thing that shook him. Conflict upset him more. For which way were he and his India to go—the way of Sevagram or Delhi? Delhi was invading Sevagram at that moment, for by order of the military department, which feared an attack on the national leaders, armed guards followed Nehru everywhere and even stood around the hut when he went into the sanctuary of the apostle of nonviolence. No wonder he opened his heart in the assembly of the followers of the Mahatma, then meeting in Sevagram, and said, "I'm confused. I don't know which way to go. The conflict is deep within me." Delhi and Sevagram fought within the soul of a highly sensitive and sincere man.

We left Sevagram and went back to Wardha. In a long interview with Dr. Rajendra Parshad, the president of the Congress, and the man who is spiritually the successor of Mahatma Gandhi, we raised this question: "Are Delhi and Sevagram incompatibles?"

He slowly replied: "You see, I'm in the same conflict. I'm committed to nonviolence, and yet there stand the armed guards at my door." The country insisted that these national leaders should not be exposed to assassination like the Mahatma, for they were not sure they had combed out all those implicated in his death, and some of these other leaders had been marked out for assassination too. He also was in deep conflict about the whole matter.

He further replied: "I think there is a *via media*. We must take the spirit of Sevagram into Delhi and leaven it. It is a pity that Bapu died before he could teach us how to live in Delhi with our principles intact."

There will be many attempts to resolve this dilemma. (1) The suggestion has been made that the capital of India be moved to Wardha and a body built that would express the soul of the Gandhian movement. Jawaharlal Nehru said in the Assembly, in reply to a question about this, that the suggested removal to Wardha was not being considered. (2) An attempt will be made to explain away the nonviolence of the Mahatma. This was done by a leading follower of Gandhi at Wardha itself when he said to me: "The Mahatma didn't rule out war. He said: 'It is better to fight than be a coward.'" But this statement of the Mahatma does not sanction war or violence; it only says it is better to fight than be a coward. If your nonviolence is only through cowardice or fear, then it is better to fight. Gandhism will be explained so that his nonviolence will be explained away, à la the Gita. (3) The Mahatma will be honored, but not followed. One of the followers of Mahatma Gandhi said as we stood in his room:

People will do to this room what the Christians have done to the cross. They will bedeck it with bejewelled spinning wheels and hang gold and silver about as a tribute to the man of simplicity. Just as you wear gold crosses instead of embodying the cross and making it your working force, we will do the same. We will honor the Mahatma and leave it at that.

(4) There will be enough people who will sincerely follow the Mahatma's spirit and ideas and will thus leaven India and perhaps the world.

Delhi is inevitable. It cannot be wiped out. For good or ill India is apparently going to be Delhized. The hope seems to be that the spirit of Sevagram will be brought into Delhi to give it a soul. If Sevagram is sufficiently vital, it can create men and women who can feed into Delhi and keep its soul alive. Like Ezekiel's vision, there can be "a spirit . . . in the wheels." The function of Sevagram is not merely to criticize Delhi, but to renew it. A saving remnant must be produced.

This saving remnant is being provided for, and is being provided for on a world scale. There met in Wardha some weeks after the Mahatma's death those who were dedicated to the continuance of his ideas and spirit. They formed two associations. One is to gather into one unit the various organizations which Mahatma Gandhi began. The other is a movement to be called 'Sarvodaya, literally, "total uplift." This movement will have no organization. It will be the projection of a spirit. Those who will inwardly accept the central principles of Mahatma Gandhi—truth and nonviolence—will be considered to belong. It will be a spiritual fraternity. Once a year as many as possible will meet in a mela, or semireligious fair, and discuss what they can do to further the spirit of the Mahatma in India and in the world. Membership will be open to anyone, anywhere throughout the world. One can send a card to the secretary, Sarvodaya Movement, Wardha, C. P., India, stating that he considers himself a member, but this is not necessary. Simple acceptance of the Gandhian principles of truth and nonviolence will automatically make him a member.

Rabindranath Tagore, India's great poet, after a trip to the West said a startling thing: "The West will accept Gandhi before the East. For the West has gone through the cycle of dependence on force and outer things for life and has become disillusioned. They

want a return to the spirit. The East hasn't yet gone through material-
ization and hence hasn't become so disillusioned as yet." He may be
right, or he may not be. Perhaps we have gone beyond Tagore's
categories of thinking and see that the East and West categories are
now outgrown; it is now just one human category. We are all in need
of just what Mahatma Gandhi emphasized. It is a human need.

Are his disciples advocating another religious cult around Mahatma Gandhi? I think not. Of course, some will deify him. Mahatma Gandhi discouraged this in life. He decried any attempt to
fasten the miraculous on him. For instance some villagers came to him
in procession with a band, and their spokesman said:

"Our village well was without water for these many years. Your sanctify-
ing footprints touched our soil yesterday, and lo, today the well is full of
water. We pray to thee—"

"You are fools!" was Gandhi's caustic interruption. "Beyond a doubt,
it was a coincidence. I have no more influence with God than you
have. . . . Suppose a crow sits on a palm tree at the moment when the
tree falls to the ground! Would you think that the weight of the bird
caused the tree's uprooting? Go back; . . . and instead of thinking about
such silly accidents, utilize your time in spinning and weaving cloth to
clothe Mother India." [1]

He discouraged any idolatry of himself. The national leaders Jawaharlal Nehru and Vallabhai Patel have both issued statements de-
ploring any tendency to set up "idolatrous memorials" to Mahatmaji.
Nor must there be any spiritual idolatry of him. As a Christian I
know where my allegiance lies. I cannot give myself to any fallible
man, even though he be as great and good a man as Mahatma
Gandhi. My allegiance is reserved for the Divine. While I give
myself to Christ and to him alone, nevertheless I can be grateful
for and can take the emphases which the Mahatma gave us. A Christianity interpreted with these emphases will be a richer Christianity.
Therefore I can say that I accept the Gandhian principles of truth
and nonviolence and am therefore a member of Sarvodaya. I think
millions will join it, for we are sick to death of war and its vast
futilities, and turn with relief and gratitude and confidence to a way
that opens the door to a new future. In the words of the historian
Toynbee: "Violence annihilates itself and leaves Gentleness alone

[1] K. Shridharani, War Without Violence, p. 246.

in the field." Gandhi was the embodiment of gentleness. He will be on the field when militarism has blown itself to pieces. For he is moral activism in political life. "He has deliberately and masterfully applied an absolute ethic to a political end with more evident purpose and larger success than any man in recorded history." "The wave of the future is Gandhism."

India must be true to Sevagram and all it stands for, and must leaven Delhi with it. I say Delhi, but one must include the provincial capitals as well. For they seem to be in greater danger of departing from the spirit of Sevagram. In Delhi there is the tried "remnant"— the national leaders who have come to the top through sacrifice and ability. The sag is at the edges—down among the lower officials.

Sevagram means "the village of service." If "the village of service" can be planted in Delhi, in every provincial capital, in every heart, then the future is secure. Gandhism wins over greedism.

But it may be that, as Acharya Kripalani said, "Sevagram will be a martyrdom." It will exist in India as a continual crucifixion. If so, then it will exist as a continual resurrection. It will have the seeds of the future in it.

CHAPTER X

Gandhi's India--The Outlook

As I took the plane to come back to India in January, 1948, I said to an Indian, a fellow traveler, "In spite of what has happened in India since the coming of independence, August 15, 1947—riots, tensions, transfer of populations, mass slaughter, upset —I look on India as the brightest spot in the postwar world among the problem areas."

He looked at me incredulously and said, "You must have been bitten by the India bug."

I assured him I had solid reasons for saying this.

India's independence came with delirious joy. Hindus and Moslems embraced each other in the streets. The battle of independence had been fought and won—and how! Never had a nation fought the battle with cleaner weapons. As I sat in the gallery of the opening session of the Constituent Assembly, meeting to draw up a constitution for the new India, I said to a friend, "Below us there sits a thousand years of jail." Added up, the jail sentences of the members of that body would have amounted to a thousand years. That tells nothing of the tens of thousands of lesser workers who had cheerfully gone to jail, but who had not reached this pinnacle of the Constituent Assembly. The Congress Movement had fought with newer, cleaner weapons, and they had earned the victory. But the dawn in the East came up blood red. There followed an indescribable period of mass killings on both sides. The delirious joy turned to gloom. How could this have happened to us? After such a warfare? I found the leaders stunned by events. They were so close to things that they could not see what really had happened. They could not see the woods for the trees. They often failed to see the whole in proper perspective. What had really happened transcended the events that followed the coming of independence. Those events tarnished the coming of independence. We must not minimize their horror, nor can they be excused. They tarnished the coming of independence, but they could not cancel the significance of it and the methods used

129

in gaining it. Moreover, these events proved the essential soundness of the Indian people when they seemed to be doing the opposite. The Indian people survived this concurrence of events which would have broken a weaker, less resilient people.

Seldom has a nation begun its career as a nation attended with a more serious concurrence of events. In a few months the nation was called on to undergo simultaneously six converging catastrophes: a revolutionary war; a civil war; two major operations when West Punjab and East Bengal were severed from the body of India; mass migrations numbering ten millions, accompanied by mass slaughter on both sides; and then, to cap it all, the tragic loss of the father of the country. Add to this the fact that the leaders of the nation were caught off balance. They did not expect to get their independence so soon. Vallabhai Patel told me that they expected to have to fight on for four or five years longer before gaining independence. Then suddenly they had to assume responsibility for the governing of the country. They had to change their mental gears overnight. Men who had been accustomed to a fighting mentality, though nonviolent, had suddenly to reverse their gears and to gear their mentality and outlook to constructive statesmanship and responsibility. The fact that they have been able to do it and to hold the country steady is a remarkable achievement. Seldom in human history has a nation, in its infancy, gone through a more difficult heartbreaking concurrence of events than India was called on to go through. In America we had a breathing space between our Revolutionary War and our Civil War. India had no such breathing space. She had to meet six converging currents that would have swept a weaker nation off its feet. The fact that India has been able to survive this assures one that she will survive anything. Having survived that, what need she fear? Someone has said that, when you raise a question, raise it in its most difficult form. Solve it there, and then you solve it all down the line. India has raised the problem of self-government in its most difficult form imaginable, has held steady amid it all, and has come out practically intact. Now she can stand anything. There is a Tamil proverb which says, "He who is born in the fire will not fade in the sun." The new India was born in the fire of six burning problems. Will she fade in the sun of the ordinary happenings? Any one of these six happenings might have broken a weaker nation, but India has survived them all. That gives me faith for the future. Having met these, she can stand anything, I feel.

Moreover, the men who were in power at the beginning of these happenings are still in power. These events would have shaken from power a weaker group. But these men in power have been tried in the fires of a great struggle for freedom. The weaker ones have been sifted out and eliminated. The survivors represent the survival of the fittest. These men at the top in the central government could be matched with any other group of officials in the world in integrity and ability and self-sacrifice. In the last named, self-sacrifice, they would go far beyond any other group.

I wish I could say the same of some of the lesser officials. Corruption and bribery have invaded the lower ranks. A man expatiated eloquently on the self-sacrifice of the Congress leaders and then, as he was about to leave the railway compartment, reached up, unscrewed an electric-light bulb, put it in his pocket, and said, "I need it," and walked out. "The average length of life of an electric-light bulb in a railway train," said the Railway Commissioner, "is twenty-four hours." Then it would disappear—stolen. I sat in the train a few days ago reading a book on Gandhiji and his amazing honesty of character. As the train stopped at a small station, at least one hundred men and women got out of the wrong side of the train, and began to run for the fields—ticketless travelers! The movement of Gandhiji reached them, but not his morals. I am told that land in East Punjab has been reassigned to refugees as many as five times, a reassignment being made each time a bigger bribe was offered. And this to refugees!

This leads me to say, though it seems a digression, that the one place where my doubts arise as to the future of this new India is at the place of character—character sufficient to sustain these outer changes. For the whole of life rests upon the imponderable thing called character. If the character breaks, the confidence breaks; and if the confidence breaks, the country breaks. The Gandhian movement was a mighty force for the producing of character. It was and is a cleansing, character-making movement. I wish I could say the same of the orthodox faiths of India. They seem to have little or no power for regeneration. They are protecting themselves instead of purifying the country. I asked a group of Indian professors what they would name as the five great needs of India and in what order of importance. They finally fastened on this list: (1) a character-producing and hope-bringing faith; (2) an economy of equal opportunity for all—economically, socially, politically, religiously; (3) communal harmony; (4) economic reconstruction—industrialization and agricultural improvement; (5) mass education—in literacy, health, corporate responsibility, character. Note that they put character first, and they put it last. They were right. For character is fundamental everywhere in East and West. And it takes a living faith to produce that character. When I talked to President Roosevelt in behalf of a group, I said to him: "You are trying to change the outer life of the country, and we are trying to change the inner, and we think that the outer rests on the inner. Therefore we think our work is not less important than yours." He nodded approval. I therefore feel that, in the making of a new India, a character-producing faith is essential. I have no hesitancy in presenting Christ as that character-producing faith. A Hindu Congressman, head of the Congress in a certain province, said as chairman of one of my meetings: "Our problem is now different. Hitherto our problem was to obtain independence. Now it is to retain it. To retain independence we need character. And there is no doubt that the impact of Christ upon human nature creates miracles of changed character. As such we welcome it in the making of the new India." Another Hindu chairman said at the close of one of my addresses: "In the future when history sums up the forces that have helped to remake this land, a very large part of the credit will go to the missionaries." Why? Because in spite of their limitations they are presenting a character-producing and hope-bringing faith. And wherever that faith is sincerely followed, character is produced. When someone asked a prominent Congressman why he seemed antichristian in his attitudes, his reply was, "I'm not antichristian. Why, the Christians are the best citizens of India." Whether that is true or not, it is interesting to note that the Christians were not molested during the rioting. The wearing of the cross gave them exemption from both sides.

Let it be said that the national leaders see this need of character, are trying strenuously to root out corruption by Anti-Corruption Departments and drives, and most of all they are illustrating in their own lives the kind of character needed. The moral sag since the war has been very great. But over against that stand these leaders at the top—incorruptible and able and strong. They will pull the country through.

Moreover, amid these terribly trying days they have been able to put through legislation to help the underprivileged in this land of underprivileged. In the Madras province they have put through legislation making it a penal offense, punishable by fine and imprisonment, to discriminate against any person in any restaurant, hotel, public conveyance, place of public entertainment, barbershop, burial ground, burning ghat, or temple, because of his caste status. At one stroke caste has been hit a mortal blow. And Madras is the home of caste! It is breath-taking.

In the new constitution of India are these words:

The state shall not discriminate against any citizen on grounds only of religion, race, caste, sex, or any one of them. In particular, no citizen shall, on grounds only of religion, race, caste, sex, or any one of them, be subject to any disability, liability, restriction, or condition in regard to (a) access to shops, public restaurants, hotels, and places of public entertainment, or (b) the use of wells, tanks, roads, and places of public resort.

There shall be equality of opportunity for all citizens in matters of employment under the state. No citizen shall, on grounds only of religion, race, caste, sex, descent, place of birth, or any of them, be ineligible for any office under the state. "Untouchability" is abolished and its practice in any form forbidden. The enforcement of any disability arising out of "untouchability" shall be an offense punishable by law.

And people are being fined for violation. In caste-ridden Malabar a teashop keeper was fined a hundred rupees for refusing to serve an untouchable. It is a far cry from that scene of a man of high caste being fined, because he refused to serve a man in a teashop, to another scene in that same section where the untouchables stood before the barrier on a road leading to a temple—a road forbidden to the untouchables—stood there, day in and day out, through sun and rain, sometimes with the water up to their waists, for a whole year in silent protest against this discrimination. They would be sent to jail, would serve their sentences, and come back and stand before the barrier. Brahmans, touched by this amazing capacity for silent suffering, joined them and also stood in protest. This moral pressure was so great that the road was thrown open. Thus the battle of Vaikom was fought and won. And now in the space of twenty years not only the roads to the temples, but the seats in restaurants—the last stronghold—have been thrown open by law. Everything is open. And the passing of the legislation created scarcely a ripple on the surface of events. A thoughtful Hindu said to me, "I didn't believe that a system, such as caste, built up through so many centuries could go down so rapidly."

Yesterday I picked up the daily paper and there were these items: (1) Dr. Ambedkar, a man from the untouchables, marries a Brahman lady. Incidentally, Dr. Ambedkar, even though he opposed the Congress Movement, was made minister for law in the new Congress government and has been the chairman of the Draft Committee to draw up the new constitution for India. An untouchable is the most important member to draw up a new constitution for India, the home of caste! (2) The Orissa provincial government, as a part of "Grow more food campaign," is offering three rupees bounty for a monkey skin. That would have been unthinkable a few years ago, for the monkey is a sacred animal and to kill one a mortal offense. But not a ripple now. It was Mahatma Gandhi who must be credited with the courage to suggest in 1928 that monkeys, if destructive of crops, should be killed. "I do not hesitate to instigate and direct an attack on monkeys in order to save the crops." This simple suggestion will, if carried out on an India-wide scale, result in saving millions annually for the peasants. (3) A man is fined in Bombay for asking an untouchable to bring his own cup for tea. (4) Ten million rupees are being spent for untouchable uplift.

And thus it goes. India is on the march. Old barriers are being swept away, and swept away overnight.

This collapse of caste was in large measure the result of the Mahatma's effort—his titanic efforts to get rid of untouchability. At one period he seemed to want to get rid of untouchability but to hold caste. But both have given way, and the most astonishing system ever built up with divine sanctions to separate man from man has fallen. It is true that pockets of resistance will remain and will have to be mopped up, but the center has given way. Caste is doomed—and doomed in its very home, India. It is now illegal, at least the discriminations based on it are illegal, and with discriminations gone the thing itself, without the bolstering of those discriminations, will die. This means that one of the greatest battles ever fought for human freedom has been fought and won, and the Mahatma led the battle. I say he led the battle, but he didn't begin it. The credit for the beginning of the battle must be given to the missionaries. As in other fields—education; medical relief; orphan, leper, and blind asylums—so in untouchable uplift they were the pioneers. They helped lift the outcastes to astonishing transformations. It was an eye opener to the nation. Then Gandhiji took up the task. He won the political freedom of 400,000,000, and he won the social freedom of 300,000,000 Hindus.

In an interview with Jinnah he began to say that there can be no co-operation with a society based on caste. I refrained from saying that there could be no co-operation with a society of theocratic fanaticism, such as is being proposed in Pakistan, based on the Shariat. I reminded him that caste is on the way out. It is doomed. It is in all stages of disintegration; but it is going down, and going down before our very eyes. I said to Jinnah: "Why base the future on the fear of something that is on its way out?" Yet he stills harps on caste, even after partition, as the excuse for not being able to cooperate with Hindus. Everything is combining to oust caste, but most of all the inner determination of the Hindus themselves.

It looks as though South Africa and parts of the United States of America, where it is still legal to discriminate against people because of the color of their skins, are to be the last remaining strongholds of caste; and both of them are democracies, and both are professedly Christian. A Hindu, professing a belief in the modified form of caste, does away with caste. Christians, professing a belief in a caste-less society, still cling to caste.

There is another battle for freedom which can be traced directly or indirectly to the Mahatma's influence. He identified himself with the poor, especially the poor peasant. He dressed and lived in identification with them. He became their living embodiment. Their hunger looked through his eyes and appealed for satisfaction. If Gandhi is India, then specifically Gandhi is the poor of India. So when independence came, one of the first things the national leaders did was lay plans to lift the weight of the zamindari system from the backs of the poor. The zamindars are the landlords who have lived at the expense of the poor tenants, squeezing out of them the last drop of blood possible. I watched the monkeys on the banks of the river at Muttra. They were clever. When the worshipers threw grain on the bank, the monkeys would quickly gather it up and stuff it in their jaws. When they had finished their portion, they jumped over and stood on the backs of the turtles which had come to the edges to get the grain thrown into the river for them. The monkeys, standing on the backs of the turtles, reached down in the water and took the share of the turtles too. The zamindars, with some fine exceptions, have cleaned up their legitimate share, and then they have stood on the backs of the peasants and have taken their share too, leaving just enough to keep them alive so they could spawn their useful kind. The peasants of India were ground between the millstones of government taxes and zamindar exactions—the most exploited peasantry of the world. If revolution came, they had nothing to lose except their debts. They were tinder for communist propaganda.

But the Congress government wisely headed off that revolution by instituting legislation abolishing the zamindari system, giving a certain amount of compensation, and returning the land to the cultivators. This was a bloodless revolution. No foreign government could have done this with such smoothness and lack of upset. It is true that the zamindars held meetings on such topics as "The Zamindari System Needs Reform, Not Abolition," but it was too late to reform. "The Devil was sick—the Devil a monk would be." It was a deathbed repentance—and too late. Some zamindars took it well. One of them said to me, "I am glad the system is gone. We zamindars will be better men—poorer, but better. We had to do things under this system that were degrading to us and to the tenants." The emancipation of the tenants, and incidentally of the landowners, was one of the great liberations of our day, and it was done in an amazingly smooth manner. This has been accomplished in some form almost all over India. The United Provinces, where the system was most cruel, was the center, and it has given way. The rest will follow. The Congress knew there was only one way to beat the communists, and that was to beat them to it, so they did. They headed off a wild revolution by a wise revolution, which will be true conservatism. Communism is not making much headway in India. Russian influence is small. [1] India wants to work out her own destiny in her own way without outside interference.

It was Mahatma Gandhi who turned the nationalist movement from a movement of the classes to a movement of the masses. Until he came, the movement was a movement of the intelligentsia, and he made it a movement of the peasantry—an uprising of the people. So when independence came, the first thoughts were for the uplift of two classes, the untouchables and the exploited peasantry. That made the movement go according to Gandhian form. To have accomplished these two revolutions in so short a time and to have done it so smoothly was a great accomplishment, and the real credit must be laid at the Mahatma's feet.

[1] See below, p. 138.

There has come into being another amazing change with independence. Admittedly the native states, comprising twofifths of India, and ruled over by Indian princes, were one of the biggest problems facing an independent India. For the most part these 562 states were feudalistic and irresponsible. The princes lived in reckless luxury at the expense of their subjects. There were some states where there was good government, but they were few. For the rest, they were a seething mass of irresponsible corruption. The British, as the paramount power, kept the princes on their thrones as long as they remained loyal and did not overstep certain loosely held bounds of propriety. Their irresponsibility can be seen in this: When the crisis came and it had to be decided whether the delegates from a certain state to the Constituent Assembly and to the Central Legislature should be appointed by the prince or be elected by the people, one prince said to his prime minister, "Oh, you know more about these things than I do. You settle it." And he went off to look after his race horses! The prime minister did settle it. All three representatives were to be elected by the people! With the backing of the paramount power gone and the people of the state electing their own representatives to the Central Legislature, where did that leave the prince? It left him high and dry! But he was so irresponsible that in a crisis he stepped out of it—into an innocuous position. The judgment hour of the princely system has come. Two years ago I was seated at a garden party in one of the largest states, given to celebrate the victory of the Allies. I remarked to a friend, "I feel that I am not in a victory celebration, but at a funeral feast. This is the end of the road. This state is resting on the bleeding backs of the poor. It can't continue. This is a funeral feast." Little did I know how quickly my remarks would come true. Like a thunder clap judgment has descended. To save themselves a semblance of position the princes have had to do two things or else abdicate: give responsible government to the people and accede to the Indian union—the union would be supreme. I am told that the proposals were put to the princes as follows: (1) there is no coercion; (2) if you sign, it will be for your good; (3) if you don't sign, you'll have to take the consequences. They signed! I did not dream that such an autocratic regime would tumble overnight. But it went down like a house of cards. The firm handling by the central government not only made the princes give responsible government to the people, but also compelled them to unite and form blocks of states to be more efficiently managed. This means that the very name and existence of most of these states are gone and their princes pensioned off. Those that remain as separate entities have been compelled to transfer power to the people. This means that the power of the princes is practically gone. At this writing I am in the last stronghold of hesitancy—Hyderabad, where a Moslem ruler, the nizam, rules over sixteen million people, of whom 88 per cent are Hindus. The state is seething. There is a pressure up from the people and a pressure down from the Indian union. The state is caught between these two millstones, and its position is hopeless, unless it does two things: gives responsible government and accedes to the Indian union—and does both quickly. Last night I sat eating with a group of splendid Christian young people in a garden, not twenty feet from which a bomb was thrown at the nizam as he passed by in a car. I came to this place over a railway where carriages were strewn alongside of the track, as a result of exploding bombs. And railway stations we passed through showed the marks of bombing, largely the work of communists. In India communism has been largely scotched by giving the land to the peasants. But in a native state like Hyderabad, where reaction is in the saddle, communism is spreading. The communists say they have "liberated" two thousand villages, the Hyderabad government no longer functioning there. To the highest officials I said yesterday:

May I quote a passage of Scripture? "Agree with thine adversary quickly, whiles thou art in the way with him; lest at any time the adversary deliver thee to the judge, and the judge deliver thee to the officer and thou be cast into prison. Verily I say unto thee, Thou shalt by no means come out thence, till thou hast paid the uttermost farthing."

If Hyderabad state agrees with the adversary quickly, then the dynasty of the richest man in the world might be saved—saved as a figurehead. Otherwise?

This state and Kashmir are the only unsettled areas. The rest are in the process of liquidation as irresponsible entities. Some of the princes have done it through patriotism to the Indian union. But the most of them have done it through the logic of events. Their day was over. The hour of judgment had come. If you had told me a year ago that within the space of eight months after independence the problem of the princely states would be practically settled by their acceding to the union, by their unification into larger units, or by their being liquidated and the princes pensioned off, I would not have believed it. Nobody would have believed it. I don't believe the Congress leaders themselves would have believed it. A miracle has happened. It has been partly the logic of events, partly the strong handling of Vallabhai Patel, partly the statesmanship of Jawaharlal Nehru, partly the pressure of the State People's Conferences, partly the patriotism of the princes, and most of all the spirit of Mahatma Gandhi. His unifying spirit was thrown into the scale of events and tipped it toward unity. A united India is emerging—has emerged. That is one of the great achievements of human history. The partition of India into India and Pakistan has, strangely enough, helped toward that unity. Two vast sections of India were taken away from India and formed into Pakistan. It was a catastrophe. But God has a way of turning catastrophe into contribution. This was expressed to me by Premier Kher after partition was decided upon: "I'm relieved. Now we can do what we want to do. Hitherto, we were hindered at every step by Moslem opposition. Now we are smaller, but we are free—to develop." India is smaller, but stronger because more unified. And the center around which India is unified is Mahatma Gandhi. His spirit pervades this union. And that spirit is healing and unifying. Just as I wrote the above, an Indian friend put into my hands a map of India with a picture of the dead face of Gandhiji at the center. The idea was that around the death of Gandhiji India is uniting. But the center of that unity is not the dead Gandhi. It is the living spirit of him that pervades it and holds it together. There are other bonds that hold it together—economic, social, cultural, political—but the spirit of the Mahatma is the living spirit of the unity.

There is another element in the making of the new India which has vast potentialities for the future, namely, the women. No greater influence has recently been poured into the public life of India than the power of womanhood. Hitherto they have been the conservative element. They have made the wheels of progress drag. One Hindu said to me, "I go into my home, and I'm in the sixteenth century. I come out, and I'm in the twentieth. I don't know to which I really belong." India has been trying to fly with one wing—the man. And she has been going around in circles. Now the Mahatma has unfastened the other wing—the woman—and India is beginning to go ahead. As in almost every department of India's life, here too the missionaries were the pioneers. They were the first to open the gates to women to enter all phases of life. Indian social reformers took up the reform. But it was the Mahatma who gave them a national task. He tapped the amazing resources of womanhood and made women a constructive force in national reconstruction.

First of all, he bravely challenged the Laws of Manu relating to women. He quotes some of these laws in his paper *Young India*:

The wife should ever treat the husband as God, though he be characterless, sensual, and devoid of good qualities. (Manu 5:154.)

The woman has no separate sacrifice, ritual, or fasting. She gains a high place in heaven by serving the husband. (Yajnavalkya 1:18.)

There is no higher world for the woman than that of her husband. She who displeases the husband cannot go to his world after death. So she should never displease her husband. (Vasishtha 21:14.)

That woman who prides in the father's family and disobeys her husband should be made by the king a prey to the dogs in the presence of a big assembly of people. (Manu 8:371.)

The Mahatma comments: "It is sad to think that the Smritis contain texts which can commend no respect from men who cherish the liberty of woman as their own, and who regard her as the mother of the race." And then he goes on and makes a bold suggestion: "There should, therefore, be some authoritative body that would revise all that passes under the name of Scriptures, expurgate all the texts that have no moral value, or are contrary to the fundamentals of religion and morality, and present such an edition for the guidance of Hindus." He again says: "I have defended Varnashrama Dharma, but Brahmanism that can tolerate untouchability, virgin-widowhood, spoilation of virgins, stinks in my nostrils."

Here is an outspoken, courageous reformer. But he was more. He threw open the gates of opportunity to women for national service and made them an integral part of the movement for national freedom. He said to a group of women in Italy: "The beauty of nonviolent war is that women can play the same part in it as men." Then again he said something still more important: "If nonviolence is the law of our being, the future is with women." Here his statement agrees with that of Benjamin Kidd, the sociologist, when he says: "Women are to be the psychic center of power in the future." Woman, when true to her function, embodies the cooperative spirit. The future belongs to co-operation; therefore woman is to be the psychic center of power in that co-operative future. It is interesting that a sociologist from the West and the Mahatma should come out at the same conclusion, and that conclusion concerns one half of the human race.

As usual he acted on his conclusion. Many have paid lip service to such ideas, but Gandhi set them to work. He put the women in service to picket the liquor shops and foreign cloth shops, to be stretcher-bearers to pick up the nonviolent wounded in the police lathee charges. And more, he gave them the same privilege of going to jail along with the men. And they went bravely and without a whimper. It is estimated that forty thousand women went to jail. Gandhi said: "The Salt campaign brought out tens of thousands from their seclusion and showed that they could serve the country on equal terms with men. It gave the village woman a dignity she had never known before."

This training in national service and in capacity to suffer has done for the women exactly what it has done for the men. The jails became the schoolrooms for the training of national leaders—at government expense! When these women came out of jail, they had to go to their inevitable place of leadership. To the credit of Mahatma Gandhi and the Congress leaders they put them in places of authority without hesitation. For instance, the deputy president of the Madras Legislative Council was a woman. And the president was an outcaste! The minister for health in the Central Government, Rajkumari Amrit Kaur, a Christian, is a gracious lady whose training was received at the feet of the Mahatma.

Mrs. Vijaya Lakshmi Pandit, sister of Jawaharlal Nehru, spent a large amount of time in jail, thus being prepared to become a minister of the United Provinces government and now ambassador to Russia, a gracious and able product of the Gandhian movement. The governor of the United Provinces, perhaps the most important of India, is a lady, Mrs. Sarojini Naidu, who spent years in jail. A nawab, a Moslem ex-ruler, during the course of a visit to Her Excellency fell at her feet, clasped his hands, and said: "Madam, please restore to me my kingdom!" This is a sight for the gods! A Moslem nawab at the feet of a woman asking for the restoration of his kingdom! And this took place in the city where the last Moslem ruler had two hundred wives, and this man was his descendant. Times change!

And now these changes are being embodied into laws. A few weeks ago Dr. Ambedkar (an untouchable!), the minister for law, moved this bill to amend and codify certain branches of the Hindu law: First, abolition of birthright and abolition of the right to property by survivorship. Second, giving a half share to the daughter. Third, conversion of the woman's limited estate into an absolute estate. Fourth, abolition of caste in the matter of marriage and adoption. Fifth, the principle of monogamy. Sixth, the principle of divorce. He said: "Under the old Hindu law, polygamy was permissible. Under the new law, monogamy is prescribed." It went through without a ripple! For it expressed the changes taking place. A couple of years ago an Indian prince made a law making polygamy illegal. He married again, leaving the princess and her eight children on the side. (Incidentally, I spoke in that palace to a royal school with Her Highness and the Crown Prince in attendance. One could see the marks of sadness in her beautiful face.) When the second wife was taken, it raised a storm of protest. The prince calmly replied: "I make laws. I do not obey them." A few years have rolled by, and now the prince does not make the laws. The people do, and the prince has to obey them. The people are sovereign. Times change!

All these dynamic changes are in contrast to what is happening in Pakistan, where the attempt is being made to found a state upon Islamic law (the Shariat). One of the first things proposed was that, since Islamic law is being enforced, all the women should go back into purdah (seclusion, behind the veil). The women raised such a storm of protest that it was quietly dropped. "The people in growing break the law, or the law breaks the people." One of the fundamental differences between Pakistan and India is this: one is attempting to base a civilization on a sixth-century, static law, and the other is attempting to base its civilization on dynamic principles. It will be interesting to see the outcome. And note that Mahatma Gandhi was at the center of this dynamic attitude. He held to the best in the past, but was not bound by the past. He was conservative, but more dynamic than conservative. Two of the greatest paralyses on the soul of India were karma and kismet—in both cases, fate. When any change was proposed, either karma or kismet stepped in and either slowed it down or blocked it. Mahatma Gandhi showed that anything can be changed that ought to be changed. He stands for moral dynamism, moral activism. He freed India from a foreign yoke, but he did more. He freed India from its real ruler: dastur, custom. He broke the tyranny of karma and kismet, a real deliverance.

A new attitude toward womanhood in India is embodied in Mahatma Gandhi. He broke down the idea of being pure by seclusion. An ascetic said to me, "I haven't seen a woman in thirty years," and he thought himself thereby pure. Mahatma Gandhi reversed all that. He was the most natural man with women I have ever seen—no prudishness, no unnatural attitudes, but complete restraint, and apparently with complete inner release and purity. Though married, he took a vow of complete continence forty years ago and kept it. At the same time he drew around him more followers among women than any other man of his age. That women are drawn only, or mainly, by the sex appeal is thereby proved untrue.

I would like to pay my tribute to the womanhood of India. Across these forty years I have been impressed with their gentleness, their devotion, their modesty, their capacity to sacrifice, their purity. The Indian woman's dress, the sari, is the most beautiful dress of the world. I hope the Indian woman never changes it for the changing fashions of Paris. If I were to pick out the one people in all the world where the relationships are the best between men and women, I would unhesitatingly pick out the Syrian Christians of Travancore, a church probably founded by the apostle Thomas. The women are equally educated with the men and move freely, but divorce is unknown, and unfaithfulness practically unknown. My salutation to the womanhood of India!

And my salutation to the Mahatma, who more than any other has brought the relations between men and women to a high, noble plane. I do not say there are no breakdowns. There are lots of them, but only as they depart from the spirit and example of the Mahatma. The father of his country has taken a fatherly attitude toward all, including women. During the Noakhali pilgrimage going from village to village after the Moslems had killed numbers of Hindus, the Mahatma came to a place where a Moslem had killed twelve Hindus. The Mahatma heard that a woman was ill in that Moslem's home. Day by day he went to see her and without a word of blame won the man over. But the astonishing thing was that the Moslem let him into his home to see his womenfolk, and the more astonishing thing was that the Mahatma should go. But it showed the Moslem's complete trust in the Mahatma concerning his attitudes toward women.

There is a sign over a women's club in Bombay: "The world was made for women too." That sign, put up years ago, can now be changed to: "The world is being made by women too." And it will be the better for their making. India is.

In the endeavors of Mahatma Gandhi to lift the people of India he saw that the incubus of drink must be lifted from the backs of the poor. So he made total abolition of liquor an integral part of his movement. This is now being put into operation in greater or less degree in all parts of the country. It is on the program for all. But they soon found that to wean the people away from drink they had to make provision for organizing the village life so that something would take the place of the liquor shops. So as a government project the villagers are being taught to play and have recreation together. They had never done so before. Life was organized caste-wise. Now they are teaching them to play and have recreation village-wise, across the boundaries of caste. This brings a sense of solidarity to the whole village. As there are 750,000 villages in India, or were before partition, this is important. It is costing the government to give up millions in revenue from liquor, but revenue coined out of the weaknesses of the poor is not revenue, but ruin.

The tide of opinion is thereby being turned against liquor as a social fashion. It is not now good form to drink in India—not since the coming of independence. When Raja Sir Maharaj Singh, the Christian governor of Bombay, came into the governorship, he announced that no liquor personally or socially would be served at Government House. The newspapers carried it on the front page, blocked off. The flood of Western influence had nearly swept India off its feet and had nearly made drinking fashionable. Now that tide has receded. It is not now fashionable to drink in India, except on the edges, in pockets of the old influence. At the center is a new determination to have a people free from this incubus. The Mahatma must be credited with this deliverance. Among his many battles for freedom this battle for freedom from tyranny of liquor was an important battle. He is winning it. Liquor is on its way out. Many a household will therefore rise up and call the Mahatma blessed.

There is another factor which must be counted among the legacies of Mahatma Gandhi: the men whom he infected with his spirit. An editorial on the death of Mahatma Gandhi in the *Manchester Guardian* said that one of the differences between Jesus and Mahatma Gandhi was that Jesus trained a group around him—the twelve—to carry on his work, but the Mahatma did not train such a group. He was unique and alone and without descendants. I disagree. Mahatma

Gandhi did not choose a specific number and train them, but he did succeed in imparting his spirit to a great number of strong men and women who are his spiritual descendants. Some of them have caught his spirit more deeply than others, but seldom has a man imparted himself to so many people on so wide a scale. And wherever you find a man who is a true disciple of Gandhi, he is a man of simplicity, of honesty, of self-sacrifice, of devotion to his country. In any movement there will be hangers-on, following for the loaves and fishes, men who dress in homespun and Gandhi cap, but their spirit is anti-Gandhi. They are using the Congress popularity for their own purposes. This is particularly true of some in provincial governments. But at the center where the leaders were in intimate contact with the Mahatma there has been created a group of people who in simplicity of life, integrity of character, self-sacrifice, and ability are the equal of any other group of men and women in public life in any country of the world. Equal? I would be inclined to put them in a class by themselves, for they have been exposed to the spirit of Mahatma Gandhi for twenty-five years and have been made different—very different. One of the first things they did when they came to power was voluntarily to reduce their own salaries to about one half of what they were entitled to. When other officials in other parts of the world do this, please let me know!

If I were to pick out two men from among the group who have been most deeply influenced by Mahatma Gandhi, I would select Dr. Rajendra Parshad, "the Gandhi of Behar," and Jawaharlal Nehru. The former was more naturally a Gandhi-ite. His spirit didn't have so far to go. He is a man of whom it could be said: "Behold, a Gandhi-ite indeed, in whom there is no guile." Jawaharlal Nehru had almost nothing naturally in common with Gandhi, nothing except a common desire for the freedom of India. They began poles apart. To Gandhiji religion was the breath of life; and while he wanted to modify Hinduism, he, on the whole, defended it. Jawaharlal on the other hand expresses himself as follows in his autobiography *Toward Freedom:*

India is supposed to be a religious country above everything else. . . . The spectacle of what is called religion, or at any rate organized religion, in India and elsewhere has filled me with horror, and I have frequently condemned it and wished to make a clean sweep of it. Almost always it seems to stand for blind belief and reaction, dogma and bigotry, superstition and exploitation, and the preservation of vested interests.

In one of the Round Table Conferences years ago Nehru said this when it came his turn to speak:

I am not a religious man. So many things are done in the name of God and religion with which I cannot agree, so I have dismissed them both from my life. I am trying to serve my country. If service to my country is religious, then I'm religious. If it is not, then I'm not.

And yet that doesn't tell the whole story, for there is a wistfulness running through Jawaharlal Nehru that makes him religious as an undertone. I said to him recently as he carried heavy burdens, too heavy for any one man to carry, "I know you are not a religious man, but I'm praying for you."

He thoughtfully replied: "Any approach that is along the moral and spiritual is a higher approach. The prayer approach is along the line of the moral and spiritual, and as such I welcome it." His wife told a friend of mine that, when Jawaharlal Nehru was despondent in jail, "he often turned to the New Testament for consolation." What he did at the ceremony of the immersion of Gandhiji's ashes at the junction of the Ganges and the Jumna is symbolic of his attitudes. The rest of the party went out in the boat to bathe ceremonially in the sacred waters while "Jawaharlal Nehru dipped his feet in the edges." That is symbolic of his wistful spirit. "I wish I could believe in God; life without him is inwardly lonely," his attitudes say.

And yet Jawaharlal Nehru was deeply attached to the Mahatma, more so, perhaps than anyone else. He bent over and kissed his feet before the flames reduced the body to ashes. That act was the homage of a devoted follower. To do that Jawaharlal Nehru had come a long way. He was not naturally nonviolent. He is a man with a temper. I feared for that temper when independence came and he had to assume the responsibilities of guiding the destiny of India as prime minister. But Nehru, the fiery fighter for independence, is now fast growing into the poised, constructive statesman. If I were to pick out the one man in East or West I would rather see go to a peace conference—a man in whose hands we could trust the liberties of the world—I would unhesitatingly pick out Jawaharlal Nehru. He would be just, and he would be courageous, and he would not bow the knee to insolent might, and he would be able. He is a man who is an intense nationalist, and yet who sees the necessity of world government—a really great man. Now that Gandhi has gone, I would choose him as the greatest man in the world today. That is no small achievement on the part of the Mahatma: to become the world's greatest man and then to produce as your nearest disciple another who, after you, becomes the world's greatest man. That is an achievement! But it is not a personal achievement. It is the direct result of the principles underlying the movement—truth and nonviolence. Both of them embodied those principles, and both of them became great. Then the credit must go to the inherent principles. That Jawaharlal Nehru did not take those principles as mere expediency, because no other weapons were available, can be seen when he said recently in reference to India's defense: "We can always fall back on the methods by which we gained independence." That is one of the most important statements made in modern India. It lifts a light for the future. The method of nonviolent non-co-operation could be used by India against any invader from anywhere and, if really practiced by the leaders and the masses, would make India invulnerable. India would be safe.

Mahatma Gandhi has wrought a miracle in the soul of this people. Forty years ago when I landed in India and came up through the country and saw the people and the countryside, I thought of one word: paralysis. I had never seen such a paralyzed people. They were paralyzed by fear, by custom, by poverty, by exploitation from within and from without, by overhanging fate—kismet for the Moslems and karma for the Hindus—and paralyzed by general hopelessness. Then thirty-three years ago Mahatma Gandhi arrived on the scene—arrived with nothing but a character and a method, both tempered in the fires of a South African struggle, a struggle which he won. When Mahatma Gandhi went to South Africa, every Indian, educated and noneducated, was called a "coolie"—"coolie teacher" or "coolie barrister." When he left twenty-three years later, that name was wiped out as a prefix. The Indians of South Africa had been raised—raised by a man and a method. Then he stepped into the paralysis called India. He quietly galvanized the soul of India into action. India began shedding her fears; timid men, and more timid women, went to jails with light on their faces. They came out and set to work renovating the country. Hope began to spring up; the light of freedom began to come into dull eyes; chains wrought through the centuries began to fall off; a new upstanding people began to emerge; a total renovation of life began to be undertaken;

a five-year plan for lifting the economic life was launched; schemes such as the Kosi Valley scheme would produce a dam longer than the Hoover Dam, the largest of the world; a tingling sense of expectancy and faith began to possess India—the renaissance of a great people was on! And freedom was won! And the architect of all this was this strange little man. He found India a fear and left it a faith; he found India a giant, bound hand and foot by Lilliputian bands, and left it a free nation; he found it divided and left it united, or on the way to unity. And he sealed it all with his own blood. In this century of great achievements Mahatma Gandhi's achievement stands head and shoulders above all others. The Russian achievement is great, but it is poisoned by its reliance on force; the American achievement is great, but it too is poisoned by turning its creative power into the production of the atomic bomb. Only Gandhi's achievement is unpoisoned. I do not mean to say that Gandhi has left a finished achievement. Far from it. There is fear in India; there is corruption in India; there is paralysis in India; but these are outside the area of the Gandhian movement, or where the movement has been corrupted by a departure from the Gandhi spirit. Where the leaders and the movement have caught the real spirit and method of Mahatma Gandhi, there is light—light for India and the world. Gandhi's India is full of promise—and hope.

CHAPTER XI

"Bapu Is Finished" -- Is He?

MANY of my readers will probably lay this book down with the feeling that they have been looking at a strange comet racing through the sky of our modern world—startling, but aloof and unrelated to the course of human events in which we live and work out our destiny. They will gasp at Gandhi and then grasp at the old discredited outworn tools. They will sigh when they do it, for they inwardly wish that Gandhi and his spirit could be made to work in our modern world. This is to miss the point. For Gandhi as a person, apart from the embodiment of certain principles, is comparatively irrelevant. He can be dismissed. But Gandhi brought to focus in himself universal principles, inherent in our moral universe. Those principles are as inescapable as the law of gravitation. Gandhi in falling was like Newton's apple falling, illustrating something universal.

What is it that Gandhi illustrates? It is this: *No individual, group, or nation need submit to any wrong, nor need they go to war to right that wrong. There is a third way: nonviolent resistance. If nonviolent resistance is organized in a thorough, disciplined way in the individual, group, or nation, then that individual, group, or nation will be invulnerable and invincible.* By taking the way of truth and nonviolence nine tenths of the possibilities of being invaded and conquered would be warded off by that very spirit. But suppose on the one tenth it should break down, and in spite of that spirit that nation should be invaded and conquered. Is all lost? Not at all. If that nation would organize its men, women, and children into nonviolent resistance, it would make permanent occupancy impossible. Let them simply withdraw all co-operation with the conqueror and take the consequences. Some would be butchered, but you cannot go on butchering nonviolent people forever. It turns your stomach. They would be the martyrs in the movement. More would be put in jail. The jails would overflow and become ridiculous. For those jailed would be the heroes of the new nation emerging. The jails would be the training ground, the schoolroom, for the new leader-

149

ship. And all the time the oppressor would become more oppressive, he would become weaker; and all the time the oppressed would resist the oppressor with this spirit, he would become stronger. It would be a losing battle for the oppressor, and he would have to succumb, converted or collapsed.

Suppose, for instance, that Russia, to take the extreme case, should invade and conquer the United States. Would we be lost? No! We could organize every man, woman, and child in America in a nonviolent resistance. We could withdraw all co-operation with the conqueror. You cannot rule over a people if they won't let you. We could break the will of the conqueror in five years. He would throw up the sponge—defeated. And in the process our nation would be strengthened in its moral and spiritual fiber, and the conquering nation would be progressively weakened. For all the time we would be hitting at the morale of the conqueror. There is something in the human heart that recoils at continuously butchering the nonviolent resisters. We would be hitting him within all the time.

If the objection is raised that this has not happened in the lands where Russia has overrun the country, the answer is that this method of nonviolent resistance has not been applied. They have sullenly submitted, or intermittently flared up in rebellion. Both methods are hopeless. But the method of nonviolent resistance would make the nation invincible. There is a way out.

What then does this mean? It means that the tensions can now be let down between nations. The hysteria can cease. We can now calmly set about removing the causes of war. We can set about building a world government under which all will be secure, including Russia. We can do it with calmness of heart, knowing that if it should fail, we can always fall back on the method of nonviolent resistance as the way out. Gandhi has lifted that light amid the encircling gloom.

When Mahatma Gandhi fell under the assassin's bullets and was carried into Birla House, a half hour later a secretary came out and brokenly announced to the stricken crowd, "Bapu is finished." The father of this country was finished. It was strangely like that cry from the cross: "It is finished." In both cases they seemed "finished." But in both cases it was just the beginning. The dramatist makes the Roman centurion say to Mary as they were taking Jesus down from the cross:

I tell you, woman, that this dead Son of yours, disfigured, shamed, spat upon, has built this day a kingdom that can never die. . . . Something has happened on this hill today to shake all the kingdoms of blood and fear to dust. The earth is his; the earth is theirs; and they made it. The meek, the terrible meek, the fierce agonizing meek are about to enter into their inheritance.[1]

The Cross was the new power that was to shake the world—and redeem it!

But the Cross in Christendom became official and artificial. It became only a sign—a sign on our churches, a charm around our necks or dangling from our watch chains, an ornament. We were no longer, save in exceptional cases, using it as a working way of life. Christendom was astray—astray at the very center of its faith, the Cross. We had turned from the Cross to material power, to imperial power, to balances of power, to atomic power. There we have come to a dead halt, frozen in our tracks, knowing that if we pursue the way of atomic power we are finished—finished as a race. We wanted power and have depended on power, and now God has had to say: "You want power. I'll have to give it to you. Look into the heart of an atom—and choose." The end of our quest for power is this: if we use it again, both sides are done for—irretrievably.

When Christendom was astray, losing the Cross in the crosses that hid its meaning, then God raised up a Hindu, protesting all the time he didn't believe in the Cross, but all the time applying it—applying it to a local difficulty in the Ashram, and applying it on a continental scale for the freedom of a nation, and revealing its power before our astonished gaze. Gandhi is our lost chord. He awakens within us a certain homesickness, a nostalgia for a kingdom which we bartered for a mess of physical power—the Kingdom of God. Gandhi the Hindu, whatever he says, calls us to the Cross.

"Bapu is finished." No, he is not finished. He is a living power—more powerful in death than in life. He will haunt our councils where we plan for power—without the Cross. He will stand in the shadows of the secret chambers where military men plan for the destruction of their enemies—and themselves and their own children. He will stand quietly by as church councils join the mad cry for war. And he will silently say, "You have forgotten something—the Cross." And,

[1] Charles R. Kennedy, *The Terrible Meek.* Used by permission of the author.

perhaps, we will listen this time, for the call of God comes from strange, unaccustomed lips.

And to India too he will come back again to haunt the councils of those who so quickly forget "the rock whence ye are hewn, and . . . the pit whence ye are digged," and turn to obvious modern gods of military power, to be like the other nations around about. India demonstrating the Gandhian way would be invulnerable, but India taking the slippery road down to militarism would be the prey of the stronger. Her strength is in the way she won her freedom—the way of truth and nonviolence. Gandhiji will be, and is, the conscience of this new India.

When I was about to go back to America just before the coming of the independence, I said to Mahatma Gandhi: "I am taking a plane tomorrow morning to America. Can you give me a message from this new India to the American people?"

"This new India?" he replied. "I am like that disciple who said: 'Unless I see in his hands the print of the nails, . . . and place my hand in his side, I will not believe.' I cannot talk about this new India until I see it actually in being, until I can touch it."

I replied: "You're right. You dare not talk about it until it is here." He seemed a great idealist, but in fact he was very much of a realist. Then I added: "Apart from this new India, can you give me a message to the American people?"

He then said: "I have not seen the American people, but give them my love." Through this book I give to the American people the love of the Mahatma. But mind you, it is not a sentimental love. It is a very stern love that would organize itself into collective action to right a wrong by taking on itself suffering. It is love facing evil, facing military might, facing injustice with an infinite capacity to take it without flinching, to return love for hate, to overcome evil with good, to overcome the world by the Cross. That is the love he sends.

But Mahatma Gandhi would send his love to Britons, too, the people with whom he fought his nonviolent warfare—his special love to them, grateful that they had something in them to which he could appeal. But he would send his love to everybody, everywhere, Russia especially, for now in his death he belongs to us all. But if we take that love, we must take its meaning, and the meaning is: "Don't give suffering. Take it." And if we do that, there need be no more war—ever. For in Gandhi we have found "the moral equivalent of war."

Suppose we should take up that simple statement of Mahatma Gandhi, "Give my love to America," and broaden it, as he would have done, into "Give my love to everybody," and suppose we should literally do it. Suppose we should, as a people—American, British, all—send out our love to the world in terms something like these:

We send you our love. And we mean it. We have no quarrel with your people. We know that you hate and fear war as we hate and fear war. We do not want to march out our young men against your young men in needless, senseless mass slaughter. We have no desire to conquer your country or any other country. We believe you have the same right to work out your destiny as we to work out ours. We hope and believe that you will reciprocate our love. If so, then war will be impossible between us, no matter what our political leaders say or do. But if a senseless madness would seize us and we should again go into war, out of which both would emerge ruined, but one a little stronger so that he would be called the conqueror, we would still not be hopeless. If you would be the conqueror, we should return to our senses and apply nonviolent resistance. Our spirit would not allow you to conquer us—for long. We should conquer you with new weapons—weapons which would strengthen us and weaken you as they were applied. But if we should conquer you in a senseless military war, then we hope that you in turn would apply to us this same nonviolent resistance. In that case you would save your freedom—and us. For in conquering you we should put ourselves in bondage to hold you down. We do not want to hold anybody down. We want everybody to be free everywhere. We send you our love—and mean it.

Suppose they wouldn't take it? Then that scripture can be applied: "As you enter the house, salute it. And if the house is worthy let your peace come upon it, but if it is not worthy, let your peace return to you" (Revised Standard Version). Give peace; and if the other receives it, then well and good; it not, then it returns to you. You are more peaceful for having given it. Give love; and you are more loving for having given it; and, even if the other doesn't receive it, you are better prepared for that final battle of spirit after military might has proved nothing, except who was physically the stronger. "Heads I win; tails I also win."

Does sending this kind of love to everybody sound sentimental? Not if we mean it. If we meant it, then it would be stark realism. I said to ten thousand young people in Cleveland a few months ago:

I know you have no quarrel with the rest of the young people of the world. You hate war as they hate war. If I could get your love past the iron curtain to the young people of Russia, would you have me say to them: "We send you our love. We do not want to be thrown at your throats any more, we believe, than you want to be thrown at ours. We have no quarrel with you. We send you our love." If I could get that word to them, would you send it?

Ten thousand young people roared their applause. And they meant it. If that could be duplicated on a wide scale on both sides of the curtain, then war would be impossible. Before this vast imponderable, military men would be powerless. For you cannot fight it; you cannot stab it; you can only succumb to it. It is the invincible. We see this more clearly now since everything I have said above has been embodied, illustrated, and demonstrated in the life and death and accomplishments of Mahatma Gandhi.

When Lincoln was shot for the same reason that Gandhi was shot, namely, for the crime of wanting to heal the wounds of a divided nation, Secretary Stanton said as he stood beside the dead leader, "Now he belongs to the ages." Of Mahatma Gandhi it can also be said, and said with deeper meaning, "Now he belongs to the ages;" for if there are to be any ages to come for man on this earth, we will have to apply his way of truth and nonviolence.

But Mahatma Gandhi doesn't belong vaguely to the ages. He belongs to this age and to the central problem of this age—this impending war.

Gandhi, therefore, is a world issue because he has lifted up a universal possibility through a universal principle, which to me is a Christian principle. Years ago Tolstoy wrote to Mahatma Gandhi in South Africa a very prophetic sentence: "Therefore your activity in the Transvaal, as it seems to us at this end of the world, is the most essential work, the most important of all the work now being done in the world, wherein not only the nations of Christendom, but of all the world, will unavoidably take part." "Will unavoidably take part!" To be able to see, in that little cloud as big as a man's hand on the horizon of South Africa, a cloud that would cover the earth and become heavy with the destinies of the race was a rare insight. But it has happened.

In this decade two forces have come to grips in a very acute form. These forces have been struggling from time immemorial, but the struggle never became so acute as now, and never before were such large stakes involved. The struggle between the material and the spiritual has now come to a head. The struggle is not really between the material and the spiritual, but between the material-minded and the spiritual-minded over the control of material forces. To what ends shall we use these material forces? The discovery of atomic energy has precipitated a crisis in human affairs greater than any other which has faced man in his long history.

One of the makers of the atomic bomb said that in three years all nations will have the knowledge of the bomb and in seven years all nations will have a sufficient backlog to destroy any other nation. He estimated that five hundred bombs could destroy America as a going unit. We have two hundred cities with populations above fifty thousand. To destroy American civilization all you would have to do would be to destroy those two hundred cities. Five hundred bombs would do it, and they need not be sent by planes, but by rocket propulsion from any part of the world, marked unerringly for their destination. And he added, there is no defense. England is even more vulnerable. That was said three years ago. Since then the atomic bombs dropped on Japan have been rendered crude in comparison to the ones now perfected. Those first bombs destroyed four square miles; those now perfected could destroy a hundred square miles, so that two hundred bombs could destroy America. Less than that number could destroy England. Another atomic energy expert says that if war starts again, both sides will be ruined in four hours. For obviously it won't start unless both sides are prepared to use atomic bombs. Add to this the fact that other forms of destruction—gas, bacteriological infection—may be used also. The outlook stuns us. It stuns us so much that it sends us into the jitters, or makes us develop an escape mentality—"Let's forget it"—or sends us to renewed efforts for a way out, a solution.

This last was the reaction of a group of scientists, makers of the atomic bombs, who called together in Chicago some of the leading Christian ministers for a two-day conference. They said in substance:

Frankly, we're frightened. We've discovered energy which we do not know how to use. We can produce the means, but we can't produce the ends for which these means are to be used. If you ministers can't produce the ends for which this atomic energy is to be used, then we're sunk. We have discovered physical power which we can't handle; it is now up to you to show moral and spiritual power which will control this energy for great human ends.

For the first time science has turned to religion and has said, "Save us: we perish." I think they were right and they were wrong in turning to the Christian ministers and dumping the problem in their lap. It is theirs, but not theirs exclusively—it's everybody's. For we are all involved in the moral responsibility, and in the physical consequences if that moral responsibility breaks down or is too feeble to guide our destiny.

It looks as though God were saying to humanity: "You are enamored of physical power; you turn to it for refuge; you make it your god; you pile up its power to defend you. Since you want it, I'm going to give it to you." And he uncovered the heart of an atom. "There is power. Now choose. What will you do with it? From now on it is co-operate or perish. You can co-operate and use this energy for making a new world for everybody, my world. Or you can use it to destroy yourselves. Now choose." And God felt the Cross press anew upon his heart as he said it.

The climax of this last war came in the dropping of the atomic bombs upon Hiroshima and Nagasaki. The dropping of these bombs was the trump card which militarism played. When they threw down this trump card on the table of events, then the game was won. Militarism won the trick and the game. The war was over. Over? Men knew instinctively that nothing was over; something had just begun. A newspaper columnist, describing the effect the dropping of the atomic bombs had on the people in Washington, said: "For three days after the dropping of the first bomb I walked the streets of Washington, and I never saw a smile on a single face. And a wisecrack would have been as much out of place as at a funeral." The bomb had not fallen on Japan alone; it had fallen on the conscience of humanity. "The Bomb That Fell on America" describes in graphic, quivering verse the dilemma in which we find ourselves. The bomb fell on us—on our consciences and on our future!

The situation following the war has steadily deteriorated. A titanic struggle is on. At the close of this war stand out two great nations, each embodying an idea—America embodying individualism and Russia embodying collectivism. Britain in the last election moved halfway between those positions. Do we fight it out to see which idea is to be top dog in the world? I hope not. For each is a half-truth. Individualism forgets that life is social, and collectivism forgets that life is individual and personal. The thesis is individualism, and the antithesis is collectivism, and now out of that clash of opposites a third something is struggling to be born, a synthesis, gathering up the truth in thesis and the truth in antithesis into a third something, a "new man out of both parties." That "new man out of both parties," the synthesis, will be a society where you love your neighbor—the truth in collectivism—as yourself—the truth in individualism. It will be a Kingdom of God society. That society is struggling to be born. Something beyond individualism and beyond collectivism is struggling to come into being—God's society, the Kingdom of God on earth. That is the meaning of this crisis. The crisis may be the death pangs of our race, or it may be the birth pangs of a new world—for everybody.

It is a dark hour—never darker. But a star has come out in the sky. The world was dark when Mahatma Gandhi fell, and it became darker after he fell. Gloom encircled us. Bernard Shaw summed it all up in a biting comment on Gandhi's death: "It's dangerous to be good." And then we saw he was wrong. It is dangerous not to be good. It is fatal. A star came out! Goodness is power! Gandhi dead was Gandhi's ideas and spirit alive—alive as never before. Immediately he became a world issue.

Gandhi stands for the power of spirit, the atma. He demonstrates the naked power of the spirit. No armies, no propaganda, no institution, no pomp, no ceremony, no outer impressiveness—just the sheer power of spirit or atma. No other human being had less of the outer and more of the inner. And because of that, no other man in his lifetime was followed by so many millions and in his death honored by so many millions more—everywhere around the world. Gandhi then raises an issue. And what is that issue? It is the issue between the atom and the atma. Will the power resident in the atom control and smash the spirit in man and all that the spirit has built up? Or will the power resident in the atma control the power resident in the atom—control it for the purpose of making a new world for everybody? We have seen the power of both—have seen the power of the atom in Hiroshima and Nagasaki, where it left piles of rubble; have seen the power of the atma in Mahatma Gandhi, where it freed one fifth of the human race and after freedom healed their divisions and gave a new hope to a confused and baffled humanity. We have seen both. The issue, then, is atom versus atma.

No other man since the world began had more physical power, including the atom bomb, under his authority than President

Roosevelt. He wielded unprecedented physical power. When the news of his death reached me, my first reaction was: "So we are having Mr. Truman!" When the news of Mahatma Gandhi's death reached me, my first reaction was: "So we are having a new era!" For Mahatma Gandhi opens to us a vista and a hope. He revives something in our bosoms. That something is the power we have seen in Jesus Christ. We have seen a Man without armies, without any of the accouterments of power, without pomp and without show, with nothing but goodness—and that goodness willing to be tortured on the cross for men—rising out of that death and resurrection to rule the hearts of men in East and West. No power on earth or heaven is anything like this. For Jesus' power survives the rise and decay of power based on force, which has its brief, bloody day and perishes. He lives on! And Gandhi, the Hindu, points us to him! I don't care what he says about it; by his life and death he points us to him! And in doing so precipitates a fresh crisis in humanity.

We have had demonstrated before us in this age, as clearly as if in a laboratory, scientific demonstration that there are three levels of life and that those three levels give certain results. The lowest level is where we return evil for good—the demonic level. The next level is where we return good for good and evil for evil—the legalistic level. The highest level is where we return good for evil—the Christian level. What are the results of living on those levels? Return evil for good, and you become evil, and then nothing in the universe backs you. The sum total of reality is against you. You quickly or slowly perish, but perish you will. Return good for good, and evil for evil, and then you become an eye-for-an-eye and a tooth-for-a-tooth person. The other man's conduct determines yours; you get your code of conduct from the actions of the other person; you have no moral standards of your own; you are an echo. When applied to nations this system leads straight to war, for you allow the conduct of another nation to determine yours. The lower-acting nation inevitably pulls down the higher-acting nation to its own level. There is war. Return good for evil, and it leads to your ennobling and to the possible redemption of the wrongdoer. In case he is not redeemed, nevertheless you are stronger.

The first level is pure weakness. The second level is semipower and pure weakness. The third level is pure power. Any individual, group, or nation that adopts it will be invincible. We believed that before; now it has been demonstrated. We have seen it before our very eyes. When we saw it demonstrated in Jesus, we were able to avoid its implications and challenge by saying, "Yes, but he was divine; we're not," forgetting that he demonstrated this power as a man. But now the challenge comes anew in a man who was very much a man—fallible, limited, originally timid, and with no special talents, except the will to act upon this level of life. And it turns out to be sheer power. He applied it on a small scale, South Africa, and won! He applied it on a colossal scale, the largest human unit but one—India—and won! He applied it to the inner unity of that colossal human unit and won! Every place and every time he applied it in its pure form, it turned out to be pure power. Alongside of the power manifested in Mahatma Gandhi the power of military might seems tinseled and irrelevant—and weak.

For we applied the greatest mass might that military forces ever applied—applied it to Europe during this last war. Result? Peace? A mess! We haven't even written a treaty of peace. And worse, we are preparing for another war as a direct result of this last war. Anything that would land us in the mess that is Europe, and that now, in the midst of that mess, compels us to prepare to do it over again, is sheer weakness—and colossal stupidity.

Hitherto we might have pleaded ignorance of the power of the spirit or atma, though we could have seen it, if we would, in Jesus. But now we have seen it in Mahatma Gandhi demonstrated before our very eyes on a colossal scale. It is no longer idealism; it is stark realism. It has been demonstrated as clearly as a problem in geometry. It is pure science.

Necessity makes strange bedfellows, so we find Napoleon and Mahatma Gandhi driven by necessity to the same conclusion. No conqueror ever gained more by wars than did Napoleon, emperor of the French, who, beginning as a poor Corsican lieutenant, for a while dominated Europe, altering boundaries, upsetting thrones. Yet Napoleon knew it was folly to rely on force. Listen to what he said, not after he had been defeated and exiled, but at the height of his success: "There are only two powers in the world—the power of the sword and the power of the spirit. In the long run the sword will always be conquered by the spirit." Napoleon dimly saw what Mahatma Gandhi demonstrated—saw that the spirit was stronger than the sword, in other words that the atma is stronger than the atom.

So Mahatma Gandhi is God's appeal to this age—an age drifting again to its doom. If the atomic bomb was militarism's trump card thrown down on the table of human events, then Mahatma Gandhi is God's trump card which he throws down on the table of events now—a table trembling with destiny. God has to play his hand skillfully, for man is free, so God cannot coerce. But God has never played more skillfully than now. He is appealing mightily to this age through the strange little man, as he has been appealing agelessly through the Man—and here the strange little man and the Man are saying the same thing: "Would that even today you knew the things that make for peace." The things that make peace do not lie in the atom and its control for military ends; they lie in the atma and its power to control the atom for the ends of a new humanity for everybody.